Study Guide

Foodservice Management Fundamentals

Dennis Reynolds, PhD

Kathleen Wachter McClusky, MS, RD, FADA

NORWICH CITY COLLEGE		
Stock No.	244 700	
Class	647. 95068	Rey
Cat.	BZ	Proc	JWL

WILEY

D1145510

This book is printed on acid-free paper. ∞

Copyright © 2013 by John Wiley & Sons, Inc. All rights reserved

Published by John Wiley & Sons, Inc., Hoboken, New Jersey
Published simultaneously in Canada

No part of this publication may be reproduced, stored in a retrieval system, or transmitted in any form or by any means, electronic, mechanical, photocopying, recording, scanning, or otherwise, except as permitted under Section 107 or 108 of the 1976 United States Copyright Act, without either the prior written permission of the Publisher, or authorization through payment of the appropriate per-copy fee to the Copyright Clearance Center, Inc., 222 Rosewood Drive, Danvers, MA 01923, 978-750-8400, fax 978-646-8600, or on the Web at www.copyright.com. Requests to the Publisher for permission should be addressed to the Permissions Department, John Wiley and Sons, Inc., 111 River Street, Hoboken, NJ 07030, 201-748-6011, fax 201-748-6008, or online at www.wiley.com/go/permissions.

Limit of Liability/Disclaimer of Warranty: While the publisher and author have used their best efforts in preparing this book, they make no representations or warranties with respect to the accuracy or completeness of the contents of this book and specifically disclaim any implied warranties of merchantability or fitness for a particular purpose. No warranty may be created or extended by sales representatives or written sales materials. The advice and strategies contained herein may not be suitable for your situation. You should consult with a professional where appropriate. Neither the publisher nor author shall be liable for any loss of profit or any other commercial damages, including but not limited to special, incidental, consequential, or other damages.

For general information on our other products and services, or technical support, please contact our Customer Care Department within the United States at 800-762-2974, outside the United States at 317-572-3993 or fax 317-572-4002.

Wiley also publishes its books in a variety of electronic formats. Some content that appears in print may not be available in electronic books.

For more information about Wiley products, visit our website at www.wiley.com.

Library of Congress Cataloging-in-Publication Data:

ISBN: 978-1-118-36334-8

Printed in the United States of America

10 9 8 7 6 5 4 3 2 1

Contents

To the Student v

PART I: THE FOODSERVICE INDUSTRY 1

Chapter 1: The Foodservice Industry 1

Chapter 2: The Foodservice Business 8

PART II: THE MENU 15

Chapter 3: Menu Planning and Development 15

Chapter 4: Recipe Standardization, Costing, and Analysis 21

Chapter 5: Menu Pricing 26

PART III: THE FOODSERVICE OPERATION 33

Chapter 6: Facilities Planning, Design, and Equipment 33

Chapter 7: Food Sanitation and Safety 41

Chapter 8: Supply Chain Management 48

Chapter 9: Food Management 56

PART IV: GENERAL MANAGEMENT 64

Chapter 10: Financial Management 64

Chapter 11: Customer Service 73

Chapter 12: Marketing 82

Chapter 13: Human Resource Management 89

Chapter 14: Leadership and Management 97

Part V: Advanced Management 104

Chapter 15: Internal Control 104

Chapter 16: Operational Analyses 112

Chapter 17: Beverage Management 121

Chapter 18: The Future of the Foodservice Industry 131

To the Student

This **Study Guide** is a companion to *Foodservice Management Fundamentals*. It serves as a resource to help you study and review the material in the text. This supplement is arranged by chapter corresponding to the chapters in *Foodservice Management Fundamentals*. We have prepared the features in this supplement to ensure that the study guide to each chapter includes resources to help you review the material, and several exercises that you can use to test your own knowledge of the key concepts discussed in the text as well as help to prepare for exams and quizzes from your instructor/professor. These resources include the following:

- **Learning Objectives**
  These highlight the key concepts presented in each chapter and provide a road map and checklist of some of the specific information that you should be learning from reading the chapter.

- **Outline**
  This provides a detailed summary of the key points presented in the chapter.

- **True / False Questions**
  A minimum of 10 (and as many as 17) true-or-false questions are provided for each chapter. These questions test your understanding of basic ideas and key concepts presented in the chapter.

- **Multiple-Choice Questions**
  A minimum of 8 (and as many as 21) multiple-choice questions are provided for each chapter. These questions ask you to choose the most appropriate response to each question. These questions ensure that you fully comprehend the key concepts covered in the chapter.

- **Fill-in-the-Blank Questions**
  A minimum of 8 (and as many as 15) fill-in-the-blank questions are provided for each chapter. These questions ask you to remember the definition and application of key terms and concepts covered in the chapter.

- **Case Activity**
  Each chapter study guide concludes with a longer, more detailed assignment that asks you to place the key concepts of the chapter within a local or personal context. These activities generally include the writing of more detailed two-page reports or essays concerning the application of these key concepts. Your instructor or professor may assign these as part of your regular class work, or you may want to complete them on your own to better understand the material by relating it to your own interests and the local marketplace.

PART I: THE FOODSERVICE INDUSTRY

Chapter 1: The Foodservice Industry

Learning Objectives

After becoming familiar with this chapter, you should be able to:

- Identify key milestones and dates in the long history of the foodservice industry.
- Appreciate the effects of culture on the evolution of the foodservice industry.
- Gain a more thorough understanding that the foodservice industry is more than just "restaurants."
- Describe the six segments of foodservice and know the factors that differentiate each one.
- Recognize the potential for enjoying a fruitful career in foodservice management.

Chapter Outline

- History
    - Roots and Ancient Origins
        - Recognize how the foodservice business arrived at its currently lofty status.
        - Food was first regarded as a commodity around 3500 BC.
        - Understand how eating, drinking, and cooking have evolved.
    - Evolution and Culture
        - Food evolved from self-preservation to nutritional, spiritual, and hedonistic satisfaction.
        - Food reflects various perspectives and values across cultures.
        - Evolution of societal norms plays an important role.
        - Foodservice industry didn't truly burgeon until the nineteenth century.
    - Foundation of Current Operations
        - Boulanger's restaurant: first advertised as *restoratives*; order from a menu.
        - The first restaurant in the United States opening in Boston in 1794.
        - In 1805, Robert Owen built a kitchen for providing wholesome meals to his employees.
        - Common features of restaurants appeared: Delmonico's introduced the printed menu and expanded into a chain.
        - The first drive-in restaurant opened in Glendale, California.
        - A new concept emerged: fast food.
    - Segmentation

- Quick Service
  - Focus is on the speed of service and low price.
  - QSRs have standardized products, an efficient delivery system, and uniformity.
  - Changes happen in supply-chain management.
  - Brand affiliation is common.
- Fast Casual
  - Fast casual has evolved from the QSR segment.
  - Responds to demand for a moderately higher quality and better ambiance.
  - Note the differences between quick service and fast casual.
- Family/Midscale
  - Table service is offered at a relatively low price.
  - Operators seek to build brand loyalty with customer-friendly programs.
  - Positioned for specific dining purposes.
  - Large portions are offered at reasonable prices.
- Moderate/Theme
  - Restaurants create a tie between the customer and a concept.
  - Restaurants have a flexible menu, knowledgeable staff.
  - Restaurants have higher prices and higher food quality.
- Fine Dining
  - Both the theme and product offering are unique.
  - Food quality and menu complexity are extremely high.
- Onsite
  - The most dynamic and growing segments are onsite.
  - Emphasis is on nutrition.
  - They must adapt to the requirements of the institutions.
  - Onsite operations must cope with longer hours and weekend crowds.

- Industry Statistics
- Managerial Implications
- Industry Exemplar: Compass Group PLC

Questions for Review

True–False Questions

1. T F Foodservice today offers more career options than ever.

2. T F In the Middle Ages, people did not pay and did not expect to pay for their own food when eating away from home.

3. T F Quick service restaurants offer more amenities than fast casuals do.

4. T F Quick service restaurants offer more flexible menu options than fast casuals do.

5. T F Midscale restaurants normally market themselves as community friendly.

6. T F Menu prices are notably lower in theme restaurants than they are in the midscale segment.

7. T F Fine dining restaurants maximize guests' overall dining experience.

8. T F Guests pay not only for the food but also for the total dining experience in fine dining restaurants.

9. T F Onsite restaurants are exactly similar to their offsite counterparts.

10. T F Compass Group PLC is the largest employer of foodservice workers on the planet.

Multiple Choice Questions

1. Which of the following was characteristic of foodservice in the Middle Ages:
   a. People never ate at their homes.
   b. People did not pay and did not expect to pay for their own food when eating away from home.
   c. Food service operators had to account for nutritional information to the customers.
   d. None of the above.

2. What was the name of the first public dining room offering a choice of dishes from a menu?
   a. McDonald's
   b. Baggers
   c. Boulanger's
   d. None of the above

3. How do segments in the foodservice industry differ?
    a. Style of service
    b. Price point
    c. Value proposition
    d. All of the above

4. What is another name for quick service restaurants?
    a. Fast-casual restaurants
    b. Fast-food restaurants
    c. Fast-paced restaurants
    d. None of the above

5. Which of the following is not a feature of QSRs?
    a. Low price
    b. Unstandardized products
    c. Efficient delivery system
    d. Limited menu

6. Which of the following differentiates fast casuals from quick service restaurants?
    a. Lack the convenience of QSRs
    b. Have fresher ingredients than traditional sit-down quick service restaurants do
    c. Involve shorter preparation time than QSRs do
    d. Both a and c

7. According to the textbook, which of the following is NOT true of family/midscale restaurants?
    a. Table service is offered, but at a relatively low price point.
    b. Brand loyalty is built with customer-friendly programs such as children's menus.
    c. Menus offer many more choices than are available in other segments.
    d. Midscale restaurants capture the narrowest possible audience compared with other segments.

8. Which of the following provide the greatest emphasis on ambiance?
    a. Moderate/theme
    b. Onsite
    c. Fast casuals
    d. Quick service

9. Which of the following have the highest menu prices?
    a. Moderate/theme
    b. Fast casuals
    c. Quick service
    d. Family/midscale

10. Which of the following focus on maximizing the overall dining experience?
    a. Fast casuals
    b. Quick service restaurants
    c. Moderate/theme restaurants
    d. Fine dining restaurants

Fill in the Blanks

1. Adults in the United States report, on average, enjoying lunch at a restaurant at least _____ every week.

2. The _____ approach to food—eating for the taste of it—spans all cultures and dates back to when we first hunted game and gathered the fruits of the land.

3. Underscoring the co-evolution of the foodservice industry with modern society, the first _____ opened in Glendale, California, in 1936 in response to the proliferation of automobiles.

4. _____ restaurants are often called *fast food* because of the speed of service.

5. Fast-casual operations offer more amenities than _____ do.

6. _____ restaurants market themselves by creating a tie between the customer and a concept based on type of cuisine or time period or some other easily captured cultural phenomenon.

7. The emphasis on the value or price of the food itself is gone; instead, _____ operators look to maximize guests' overall dining experience.

8. _____ foodservice firms must adapt to the requirements of the institutions within which they operate.

9. The _____ industry employs more minority managers than any other industry does.

10. The _____ and even therapeutic value of the food is today considered a vital component of the holistic process of patient care.

Case in Point: This Isn't What It Was Like When I Was in College

Both of Katlin's parents had graduated from Central State University, so they were very excited when Katlin listed it as her first choice for college. They were also ecstatic about visiting the university for a tour. Katlin's mom, Kathy—a graduate of the university's hospitality program—had been reminiscing almost nightly about her college days and was curious to see how things had changed. Her father, an architect named Sam, was also curious about the changes they would see on campus.

Because the visit to her parents' alma mater would include meetings with some of the faculty and the hospitality program's adviser, Katlin began preparing a list of questions in anticipation of her encounters with potential future professors. Although she was curious, of course, about the curriculum, she was somewhat familiar with the general program thanks to the hours she had spent perusing the various CSU online sites. She wondered which companies typically recruited new graduates. How much money could she anticipate making as a new hire? What other choices would she have after graduation?

Katlin knew what she wanted to do with her college degree but she was worried that her goal might disappoint her parents, so she kept it to herself. This made the last few weeks leading up to the college visit a little awkward during family dinners. Sam and Kathy assumed that her silence meant that Katlin didn't know what she wanted to do. They were worried that she wouldn't seem focused on a clear goal during the meetings at CSU.

Throughout the drive to the small college town, Kathy talked about all her college friends who had gone on to work in hotels when they finished college. Kathy herself had started with a large hotel chain with whom she had worked for many years before starting her own travel agency. Sam had just finished designing some high-end restaurants, so his mind was more on Katlin's opportunities in the foodservice sector. Katlin's parents dropped subtle hints (well, maybe some were not so subtle), hoping to elicit from Katlin some indication of her desired career path, but Katlin just nodded and smiled politely.

After meeting two of the professors and the academic adviser, the trio met with the hospitality school's director. The conversation was casual at first, but the small talk soon gave way to a more pointed inquiry when the director looked Katlin square in the eye and asked, "So what do you want to do after you graduate from CSU with a degree in hospitality management?"

Sam and Kathy held their breath. Katlin, meanwhile, inhaled loudly and said, "Last year in school I found Fannie Merritt Farmer's *Boston Cooking School Cook Book,* which my English teacher described as "the Bible of the American kitchen." He said that it changed the way cookbooks were written forever by listing exactly how much of each ingredient would be needed at the top of every recipe. Then she gave the instructions for making the dish. I thought that was amazing. But what I found even more amazing is that many of the dessert recipes from this book, which was written way back in 1896, are a lot like many of today's recipes."

Katlin continued: "That got me interested in baking—especially in trying new things, using new ingredients, and applying different approaches. And I do enjoy this, but my passion isn't only for baking. I want to redefine bakeries as a *business*. So, my goal is to start a chain of high-end bakeries, starting maybe with my first one in New York City and then adding a few more each year. I'm hoping this program will enable me to do that."

Sam and Kathy just stared at Katlin. They had no idea that she was so focused or that she had such an ambitious goal. On the other side of the desk, the director grinned widely. He then responded, "Well, I must tell you how refreshing this is. Too often, students look at managing a single restaurant or hotel, or working with an event-planning business. You, on the other hand, want to be an entrepreneur. And that is exactly what we're designed to foster. In fact, our collective mission in the school is to craft our best and brightest into the leaders of the global hospitality industry. I have a feeling that you will be at the front of our next cohort of these leaders."

Did you have a similar experience when you were considering which college to attend or maybe deciding if dietetics or hospitality was in your future? How would you have responded to the same director if you were Katlin? And now that you're in a hospitality or dietetics program, how would you respond today?

Chapter 2: The Foodservice Business

Learning Objectives
After becoming familiar with this chapter, you should be able to:
- Understand the unique aspects of the foodservice business including its characteristics and distinct segments.
- Relate current trends to foodservice operations' evolution throughout the business lifecycle.
- Appreciate the importance of site selection and the value of environmental scanning in terms of the foodservice marketplace.
- Describe value as it is perceived by guests, integrating the various components of the overall dining experience.
- Discuss value drivers, along with the role of capacity constraints and the importance of understanding the service-value chain.

Chapter Outline
- What Makes the Foodservice Business Unique?
  - The foodservice business and the accompanying business landscape are incredibly diverse.
  - The type and quality of serviceware vary.
- Key Characteristics
  - Sales volatility
  - Product perishability
  - Labor intensiveness
- Trends
  - More serving size options, including small plates
  - Children's menus offer truly unique menu items
  - How to acquire information on trends
- Business Lifecycle
  - Restaurant lifecycle stage (Figure 2.1)
  - Industrial features and operational strategies for each stage
- Understanding the Marketplace
  - Environmental Scanning
  - Concept mapping (Figures 2.2, 2.3, 2.4)

- Value from the Customers' Perspective (Figure 2.5)
  - Value Drivers
  - The Service-value Chain (Figure 2.7)
  - Capacity Constraints
- Managerial Implications: Maximizing Opportunities in the Competitive Marketplace
- Industry Exemplar: Papa Murphy's
- Case in Point: Restaurant No. 2

Questions for Review

True False Questions

1. T F In the foodservice industry, it is important to identify what may now be just a fad but will later become a trend.

2. T F In the introduction stage of the business lifecycle, there is intense focus on resource management.

3. T F In the maturity stage of the business lifecycle, operations are streamlined.

4. T F In the decline phase of the business lifecycle, management must renew its knowledge of the market and its customers' consumer preferences.

5. T F Understanding an area's economic situation before starting a restaurant is part of concept mapping.

6. T F Mimetic isomorphism is the tendency of firms in a market to become more like each other.

7. T F The most obvious capacity constraint in the restaurant business is the number of seats.

8. T F Exploring the competitive marketplace by individual type of cuisine is a critical step in concept mapping.

9. T F Environmental scanning potentially offers a sustainable competitive advantage to a firm looking to enter a market.

10. T F Seasonality is not a characteristic of sales volatility.

Multiple Choice Questions

1. Which of the following is NOT a characteristic of sales volatility?
   a. Seasonality
   b. Day-to-day sales
   c. Intraday volatility or daypart volatility
   d. Product perishability

2. Which of the following is NOT a characteristic of the foodservice business?
   a. Product perishability
   b. Labor intensiveness
   c. Sales volatility
   d. None of the above

3. Which of the following is NOT a stage in the business life cycle?
   a. Rebirth
   b. Decline
   c. Growth
   d. Maturity

4. Which of the following is part of the growth stage of the business life cycle?
   a. Determine an establishment's price-value position.
   b. Sales stabilize and the brand becomes fully leveraged.
   c. There is an intense focus on resource management.
   d. Localized markets are emphasized.

5. Which of the following is NOT a key value driver affecting customer choice in foodservice business?
   a. Price points
   b. Location
   c. Personal service
   d. None of the above

6. Which of the following is NOT a driver of customer equity?
   a. Value equity
   b. Brand equity
   c. Retention equity
   d. None of the above

7. Which of the following can be a capacity constraint?
   a. Parking
   b. Number of seats
   c. Labor
   d. All of the above

8. What is true of the understanding of value from the customer's perspective?
   a. Originally, value was understood as a simple function of price.
   b. It is not an important concept in the restaurant business.
   c. A more holistic definition of value evolved later, incorporating customer expectations, service, and atmosphere into the original definition.
   d. Both a and c.

9. Which of the following is the basic premise behind concept mapping?
   a. Identify possibilities and exploit untapped opportunities.
   b. Understand an area's economic situation.
   c. Both a and b.
   d. None of the above.

10. What phenomenon is revealed when concept mapping is performed routinely over time in the same marketplace?
    a. Environmental scanning
    b. Capacity constraint
    c. Sales volatility
    d. Mimetic isomorphism

11. In terms of marketplace assessment, the list of capacity constraints starts with the number of potential customers. What is a basic approach to calculating this figure?
    a. Calculate the number of seats available versus the number of potential guests in a given subsegment.
    b. Undertake environmental scanning.
    c. Calculate the number of seats available versus the number of employees in the restaurant.
    d. None of the above.

12. Which of the following is a utility of the service-value chain?
    a. It paints a fuller picture of the ways in which restaurant concepts differ from one another.
    b. It aids in analyzing the competitive marketplace.
    c. It helps foodservice managers understand value from many perspectives.
    d. All of the above.

13. The service-value chain ends with which of the following?
    a. Customer satisfaction and customer equity
    b. Employee retention and employee productivity
    c. Revenue growth and profitability
    d. None of the above

14. What is the name of the concept that denotes the customer's objective assessment of the utility of a brand, based on perceptions of the value of what is given up relative to the value of what is received?
    a. Brand equity
    b. Value equity
    c. Retention equity
    d. None of the above

Fill in the Blanks

1. _____ volatility lays the foundation for such familiar offerings as early bird and happy hour specials.

2. A _____ is a small portion, usually a quarter of a full-size menu offering.

3. Today, _____ menus offer truly unique menu items—no longer just chicken fingers and grilled cheese sandwiches with fries.

4. At the _____ stage of the business lifecycle there should be a strong investment in advertising in order to penetrate the market.

5. Menu refinements continue at the _____ stage of the business lifecycle, but the emphasis is generally on high-profit items.

6. The most useful first step in understanding a market composed of various foodservice operations is a process known as _____.

7. As defined in the *International Encyclopedia of Hospitality Management*, _____ is a technique that provides the fullest possible understanding of relationships among ideas, concepts, and even business operations.

8. _____ is the tendency of firms in a market to become more like each other.

9. _____ are organizational capabilities that can be used to enhance value to the guest.

10. _____ is the strength (and value) of the relationship between the customer and the organization or brand.

Case in Point: Restaurant No. 2

Kris Mueller had already realized considerable success with her first restaurant in a bustling suburb of Orlando, Florida. But she had been lucky. Since she had very limited resources, she had not been picky about the location and had accepted an offer from a family friend to launch her concept in the strip mall he owned. To be sure, she realized that most locals went to the new mall with the high-end anchor stores just a few blocks away, but she really didn't have much choice. Besides, it had worked out fine. After 15 months of operation, she was showing a profit and already had an investor interested in helping her launch a second unit.

The investor was, however, rather restrictive regarding his offer to help. He would cover all start-up costs, but would terminate the relationship if Kris could not show strong cash flow from the new operation within the first two quarters of operation. Furthermore, he wanted her to open the new unit in Tampa, a very different setting from the one she had chosen and one about which Kris knew very little. The investor explained that he selected Tampa because that was the location of his main office and he felt the convenience of being nearby would help him entice investors to launch the concept as a national chain.

Even with her limited experience in restaurant ownership, she knew this meant that she needed more than luck to start the second unit. She had been to Tampa once and even had a distant aunt who lived there. How could she learn about the market quickly to assess whether her concept would make it?

Around that time, Kris remembered a college friend who had joined a hospitality consulting firm after graduate school. She called Lucy, and, after reminiscing with Lucy about the good old days, she posed the question: Can you help me assess the area of Tampa where I'm hoping to open the new restaurant?

Kris was rather startled by Lucy's response. Lucy explained that her company used complex analytical tools designed for various types of service-based businesses that could provide useful information. Furthermore, she had just completed a similar analysis for another client with surprising results. As a friend, Lucy disclosed to Kris that she had recommended to her client that he not open a restaurant there! Lucy went on to say that this client's value proposition was similar to the one offered by Kris's concept.

After thanking Lucy with a guarantee of free desserts for life at her restaurant, Kris called her potential investor. Without divulging the confidential information she had received from Lucy, she explained to him that she thought it was a bad idea to open in the area near his office. She added that she would be interested in considering another location.

The investor reiterated that he needed the new restaurant to be near his office. "Kris, don't you want me to take all my wealthy clients there?" he asked. The conversation ended with a clear message to Kris: If you want my money, you'll open the restaurant near my office. If not, then consider this relationship ended.

Kris stared out the window, gripped by a sense of impending doom. Should she take the shot and gamble on success? Or, should she listen to her friend's free advice and wait for another chance—one that might never materialize?

PART II: THE MENU

Chapter 3: Menu Planning and Development

Learning Objectives

After becoming familiar with this chapter, you should be able to:

- Appreciate the importance of menu philosophy.
- Understand the basics of menu planning and review the importance of the menu in any foodservice operation.
- Recognize how menus differ across the various segments of onsite foodservice.
- Be able to explain the art underlying menu development.
- Identify and explain differences in menu philosophy as they apply to sustainability.

Chapter Outline

- Philosophy

- Planning

  - Planning and Development Phases

    - o Foodservice menu requires careful strategic planning.

    - o Factors that predominately influence menu planning (see Figure 3.1).

    - o Menu label requirements require food establishments with 20 or more locations to list calorie content information in their menus.

  - Categorization and Menu Policy

    - o QSRs

    - o Fast Casual

    - o Family/Midscale

    - o Moderate/Theme (Figure 3.5)

    - o Fine Dining

- Menus in Onsite Foodservice

  - Healthcare

    - o Cycle menu is a rotating menu over 6 to 30 days (Figure 3.7).
    - o Selective cycle menu includes choices (Figure 3.8)
    - o Room service is a growing trend in healthcare foodservice.

- Schools
  - The National School Lunch Program provides nutritionally balanced, low-cost or free lunches for schoolchildren.
  - Nutritional requirements for school lunches (see Figure 3.12).
- Colleges and Universities
  - NACUFS is composed of member foodservice operations.
  - The mission of operations describes the basics of foodservice in higher education.

- Business and Industry

- Sports and Recreation

- Correctional Facilities

- The Art of Menu Development

- Sustainability in Menu Planning

- Industry Exemplar: Seasons 52

- Case in Point: The Handwritten Menu

Questions for Review

True False Questions

1. T F   Table d'hôte is a menu that offers single-course meals with unlimited choices at variable prices.

2. T F   *À la carte* refers to a menu of items priced and ordered separately rather than selected from a list of preset multi-course meals at fixed prices.

3. T F   The physical environment in a QSR truly focuses interest on the "menu display."

4. T F   Family/midscale restaurants target the customer who's in a hurry.

5. T F   Many fast-casual restaurants are marketed as health-conscious.

6. T F   Quick service restaurants often involve "fusion cuisines" to increase interest or variety.

7. T F   Ethnic themes make up the largest segments in moderate/theme restaurants.

8. T F   Healthcare menus reflect the patient-care philosophies of their institutional hosts.

9. T F   In sports and recreation, operators must identify items that create value in terms of the item's quality or unique attributes.

10. T F   A cycle menu is a menu on which the offerings are planned for a period of from 6 to 30 days and then are repeated at the end of that period.

Multiple Choice Questions

1. Which of the following is NOT a consideration in the major types of hospital diets and menu-planning?
    a. Regular or house or general menu
    b. Special or modified menu
    c. Consistency modifications
    d. None of the above

2. Which of the following is NOT true of a selective cycle menu?
    a. It usually includes two entrees only with no sides, dessert, or beverage.
    b. The diner receives the menu for the next day and indicates his choices.
    c. The risk of repetition is even greater when the planner must include at least two items for every meal.
    d. Even with the choices offered under this scheme, it is often the case that the diner does not like either choice.

3. What was once the most common format of foodservice operation in business and industry?
   a. Room service
   b. Cafeteria-style
   c. Kiosk-style, walk-up-and-order with a limited menu
   d. Take-out

4. What types of restaurants are often ethnic in nature?
   a. Moderate/theme restaurants
   b. Fast food restaurants
   c. Family/midscale restaurants
   d. Both a and c

5. Which of the following has shaped the development of onsite foodservice menus and operations?
   a. Wellness
   b. Sustainability
   c. Nutritional content
   d. All of the above

6. Who usually plans a special or modified menu?
   a. Registered dieticians
   b. Physicians
   c. Customers
   d. All of the above

7. Where can one find the definitive guide to daily nutrient needs?
   a. The U.S. Department of Agriculture (USDA) Food and Nutrition Service
   b. The Center for Medicare Services (CMS) of the US Department of Health and Human Services
   c. The Recommended Daily Allowances of the Food and Nutrition Board of the National Research Council of the National Academy of Sciences
   d. None of the above

8. Which of the following is NOT a characteristic of quick service restaurants?
   a. There are multiple locations for ordering.
   b. The physical environment truly focuses interest on the "menu display."
   c. QSRs often involve a selection of breads, soup, or salad included with an entree, and/or salad bar.
   d. None of the above.

Fill in the Blanks

1. The _____ menu expands on the QSR concept by enhancing each of the key features of a QSR while still providing value for the dollar.

2. A _____ is a cycle menu including choices, usually two entrées paired with various sides and perhaps a choice of fruit or dessert and a beverage.

3. The composition of a healthy diet is summarized in the USDA's _____.

4. The _____ of the US Department of Health and Human Services publishes a highly detailed manual of "Operational Guidelines" for Residential Care.

5. _____ is a federally assisted meal program operating in public and nonprofit private schools and residential childcare institutions.

6. _____ is a concept that applies to menu planning and allows a wider range of lunches to be considered reimbursable under NSLP guidelines.

7. According to the website of the Division for Sustainable Development of the United Nations Department of Economic and Social Affairs, _____ is a "development that meets the needs of the present without compromising the ability of future generations to meet their own needs."

8. The concept of _____ has been used to describe the distance that food has to travel before purchase by the end customer.

9. One of the best guidelines for sustainability is the Monterey Bay Aquarium's _____, which helps the consumer and foodservice operator identify which seafood choices are sustainable and which are not.

10. In a _____ restaurant, the menu is the focal point for customers and its items are designed for quick, efficient preparation.

Case In Point: The Handwritten Menu

This chapter has looked at the menu as a management tool. The menu is, however, also a marketing tool for any foodservice operation. There is a small, chef-owned restaurant in a coastal town in the Northeast. At this small restaurant, the chef shops every morning at the docks for fresh fish and at local markets for produce and other items. He then handwrites four or five menu items on a plain piece of paper. He will do this 10 times—there is no copy machine or printed menu. The server brings one of the handwritten pieces of paper to the table—since there are few copies, diners have to make their choices quickly so the menu can be passed on to others. There are no additions, and no substitutions are allowed by the chef. The menu is rather messy and hard to read. Despite the chef's rather unusual personality, the "locals" flock to the door at dinner. Oh yes, the phenomenal view of the ocean probably attracts them as well!

Discuss how this chef follows or ignores the principles of menu planning outlined in this chapter. What unusual factors can you identify in this scenario that could account for his success? Would you suggest that this chef/owner change his menu style or philosophy? If so, why? If not, why not?

Chapter 4: Recipe Standardization, Costing, and Analysis

Learning Objectives:

After becoming familiar with this chapter, you should be able to:

- Understand and appreciate the importance of recipe standardization.
- Explain the basic methods of recipe standardization.
- Explain the methods used to calculate a recipe's cost.
- Appreciate the purpose and use of recipe analysis.
- Identify all major issues are involved in accurately costing recipes.
- Understand the role of computer software in all of these processes.

Chapter Outline

- Recipe Standardization
  - Definition
    - o Steps for standardizing recipe
  - Advantages and Disadvantages
    - o Procurement planning, fiscal planning, scheduling, teaching, nutritional analysis, chemistry, extensions and mise en place
    - o Cost, training issues, creativity issues, communication, computers and quality
  - Chefs and Dietitians
    - o Five credentials for chefs
    - o Seven credentials for dietitians
    - o The role of chefs and dietitians
  - Applying Yields
    - o Definition of yields
    - o Reasons for the importance of yields
  - Development and Standardization (Figure 4.1)
- Recipe Costing
- Recipe Analysis
  - Nutritional Analysis
  - Intake Analysis
  - HACCP
- Summary
- Industry Exemplar: Morrison
- Case in Point: Recipe, What Recipe?

Questions for Review

True False Questions

1. T F A registered dietitian *must* have an undergraduate degree in nutrition or dietetics or the equivalent in coursework from an accredited institution and must pass a standardized exam developed by the Commission on Dietetic Registration (CDR).

2. T F A food yield is an equivalent measure of a specific food.

3. T F Recipe costing is the process of determining the major nutrients in one serving of an item.

4. T F HACCP stands for Hazard Analysis Critical Control Point.

5. T F The US Food and Drug Administration (FDA) does not include HACCP guidelines in its regulations covering foodservice facilities.

6. T F Intake analysis determines the content of foods that are actually consumed by individuals.

7. T F In recipe costing, a *unit of measure* provides a basis on which a person or a computer can calculate the price of an item correctly.

8. T F In the "Cooking Professionals" category of the certifications offered by the American Culinary Federation (ACF), there are seven credentials based on education and work experience requirements.

9. T F A Certified Sous Chef ™ (CSC™) has demonstrated the highest degree of professional culinary knowledge, skill, and mastery of cooking techniques.
10. T F Yield tables have no use when applied to developing or changing a recipe.

Multiple Choice Questions

1. Which of the following should be included in a standardized recipe?
    a. Total time for recipe preparation and cooking time
    b. Amount of time involved in each preparation step
    c. Food items, listed in order of use
    d. All of the above

2. The development of a standardized recipe, through several steps of testing and adjustment, is known in management as _____
    a. A complicated process.
    b. An iterative process.
    c. A one-step process.
    d. None of the above.

3. What is the process of determining the major nutrients in one serving of an item?
    a. Recipe costing
    b. Yield analysis
    c. Unit of measure
    d. Recipe analysis

4. In healthcare or residential care settings, the dietitian and the medical team must plan for care based on what?
    a. Patient's words
    b. Intake analysis data
    c. Profitability
    d. None of the above

5. Which of the following is an example of an HACCP guideline?
    a. Determination of an establishment's price-value position
    b. Storage temperatures
    c. Recipe information
    d. None of the above

6. _____ includes HACCP guidelines in its regulations covering foodservice facilities?
    a. The American Culinary Federation (ACF)
    b. The Academy of Nutrition and Dietetics
    c. The Commission on Dietetic Registration (CDR)
    d. The US Food and Drug Administration (FDA)

7. Which term denotes the process of preparing and arranging all the ingredients in a recipe so that they are ready to be combined efficiently to produce the desired item?
    a. Extension
    b. À la carte
    c. Mise en place
    d. None of the above

8. Which is NOT one of the five credentials based on education and work experience requirements in the Cooking Professionals category offered by the American Culinary Federation (ACF)?
    a. Certified Culinarian
    b. Certified Sous Chef
    c. Certified Chef de Cuisine
    d. Certified Dietician

9. Which of the following is NOT an advantage of using standardized recipes?
   a. Fiscal planning
   b. Procurement planning
   c. Communication
   d. Scheduling

10. Which of the following is NOT a disadvantage of using standardized recipes?
   a. Training issues
   b. Creativity issues
   c. Cost
   d. None of the above

Fill in the Blanks

1. Without _____ a manager cannot determine what foods to purchase to produce a given recipe or how long it will take to produce the item, nor can she be sure that it will be correctly prepared.

2. A food _____ is an equivalent measure of a specific food.

3. A _____ provides a basis on which a person or a computer can calculate the price of an item correctly.

4. The development of a standardized recipe, through several steps of testing and adjustment, is known in management as an _____ process.

5. _____ is the process of determining the major nutrients in one serving of an item, which is accomplished by determining the amount of each nutrient in a given quantity of each ingredient.

6. _____ determines the content of foods that are actually consumed by individuals.

7. Food safety is achieved through the application of a system known as _____.

8. A _____ has demonstrated the highest degree of professional culinary knowledge, skill, and mastery of cooking techniques.

9. The _____ is the world's largest organization of food and nutrition professionals.

10. _____ is a French culinary term that denotes the process of preparing and arranging all the ingredients in a recipe so that they are ready to be combined efficiently to produce the desired item.

Case in Point: Recipe, What Recipe?

Having just graduated with a college degree, Tim was excited about his new job at the city's newest dinner house. Tim had interviewed with the two owners—Bill and Bonnie, a husband and wife team—and knew he could make a difference managing their small dining room. The owners made it clear that their strength was in the kitchen (both were experienced chefs) and that what they needed was someone who could take care of the front of the house. Bill and Bonnie were honest with Tim and explained that, not long after the restaurant had opened only a few weeks earlier, they realized that they couldn't manage all aspects of the operation themselves. They hoped to divide the kitchen duties so that while one was cooking the other could focus on administrative matters like paying invoices, processing payroll, and compiling financial information. Ultimately, the owners wanted to open a chain of restaurants with the same menu, décor, and so on.

The first few nights were great. The customers raved about the food and generally enjoyed the dining experience. There was the occasional glitch with food coming out of the kitchen a little slowly when all the tables were full, but after the initial rush everything was running pretty smoothly. At the end of each night, Tim sat with Bonnie and discussed how they could change things to improve the speed of service and coordination between the kitchen and the dining room staff.

On the fourth night, Tim began hearing complaints about the food. Some complained that the portions were too small; one couple who had been at the restaurant the week before asked why they had changed menus. Tim couldn't understand what was happening. He made it through the night, but ended up not charging several guests for their meals in response to their numerous complaints.

This was the first night Tim had worked with Bill only (it was Bonnie's night off). As soon as Tim began to explain the nature of the complaints, Bill became defensive. Tim was careful not to criticize the food or the preparation but tried to explain that he had received no complaints during the previous evenings. Bill and Tim agreed that it was probably a fluke and that they would consider the evening a learning experience. Unfortunately, the next night was exactly the same. The main complaint was about portion sizes; guests felt they were being overcharged for the small portions and many told Tim that they would not return.

Finally, at the end of that night, Tim asked Bill the fateful question: "Are you using the same recipes that Bonnie uses?" Much to Tim's surprise, Bill didn't get upset. In fact, his first reaction was a big smile. Bill said, "My wife and I have different styles, but we agreed on menu items that complement both our talents. We don't always see eye to eye on some of the sauces, so these might change from night to night. She also tends to use more meat than I do. Between you and me, I think she's trying to give away the house with her large portions, but I figure we balance each other out doing it this way."

Tim drove home wondering what to do. He certainly didn't want to create problems between Bill and Bonnie, but he knew that without consistency the restaurant would not be successful. What should Tim do?

Chapter 5: Menu Pricing

Learning Objectives

After becoming familiar with this chapter, you should be able to:

- Understand the major menu pricing approaches.
- Explain the methods used to calculate a menu item's price.
- Appreciate the importance of menu psychology and understand how it applies in the menu development process.
- Recognize the importance of menu engineering and understand how various approaches can be applied.

Chapter Outline

1. Pricing Approaches

   - Nonstructured

   - Factor Method

   - Prime-Cost Method

   - Actual-Cost Method

   - Gross-Profit Method

   - Stochastic-Modeling Approach

2. Menu Psychology

   - Design

     o Align with the operation's theme

     o Uniqueness and readability

   - Communication (Figures 5.4, 5.5, 5.6)

     o Price

     o Item description

     o Humor

     o Honesty

   - Truth and Accuracy

     o Consistencies between menu descriptions and the actual items served

     o Truthfulness of menu descriptions for vegetarians

     o Nutritional information

- Extending Menu Philosophy
  - Bundling

  - The children's menu

  - The cocktail menu

3. Menu Engineering (Figure 5.8)
   - Origins
     - Two key variables: gross profit and popularity
     - Analytical deficiencies
   - Advanced Techniques
4. Industry Exemplar: Applebee's
5. Case in Point: The $47 Burger

Questions for Review

True False Questions

1. T F Nonstructured pricing is the most complex approach to menu pricing.

2. T F In the factor method, a factor is established by dividing 1.0 by the desired food-cost percentage.

3. T F The factor method does not reflect the potentially differing labor costs associated with dissimilar menu items.

4. T F The prime cost method does not reflect cost differences that distinguish labor-intensive items from prepared foods.

5. T F The actual cost method limits an operator to information found on the operation's pro forma statement.

6. T F The gross profit method underscores the importance of pricing menu items on the basis of how many are expected to sell.

7. T F Customers tend to round a price of $9.95 to $10 rather than $9.

8. T F Bundling represents discount pricing and convenience for the customer.

9. T F Cocktail menu designers should always feature basic drinks such as gin and tonics.

10. T F Menu mix is the type and number of offerings in each menu category.

Multiple Choice Questions

1. Which of the following is a driver of menu pricing?
   a. Market
   b. Demand
   c. Both a and b
   d. None of the above

2. Which menu-pricing option can be adopted more robustly for customers who want items or service styles for which there are few providers or alternatives in the marketplace?
   a. Market-driven pricing
   b. Demand-driven pricing
   c. Both a and b
   d. None of the above

3. Which of the following is the easiest pricing approach?
   a. Nonstructured pricing
   b. The factor method
   c. The prime cost method
   d. None of the above

4. Which of the following consists of little more than a cursory examination of the competition's prices with no consideration of other factors?
   a. Nonstructured pricing
   b. The factor method
   c. The prime cost method
   d. The gross profit method

5. A restaurateur visits two restaurants with themes similar to his and prices his menu to approximate the prices charged for similar dishes at the other restaurants. What menu pricing tactic did he use?
   a. Nonstructured pricing.
   b. The factor method
   c. The prime cost method
   d. The actual-cost method

6. Which pricing tactic is most commonly used in the foodservice industry?
   a. The prime cost method
   b. The factor method
   c. The stochastic method
   d. The gross-profit method

7. Which of the following accomplishes the vital goal of including profit in the price of every item on a menu?
   a. Nonstructured pricing
   b. The factor method
   c. The prime cost method
   d. None of the above

8. Which of the following requires that labor costs be separated into direct labor costs and indirect labor costs for each menu item?
   a. The prime cost method
   b. The factor method
   c. The stochastic method
   d. The gross-profit method

9. What are direct labor costs?
   a. Labor used to finish an item, such as grilling or frying
   b. Labor used for the preparation of a specific menu item
   c. Labor used in serving food only
   d. None of the above

10. Which of the following is NOT included in the pricing calculation based on the actual-cost method?
    a. Food cost dollars
    b. Total labor cost per guest
    c. A related variable cost percentage
    d. None of the above

11. What is the best pricing method to use for situations such as catered events?
    a. The factor method
    b. The prime cost method
    c. The actual cost method
    d. The gross profit method

12. Which of the following is NOT one of the data necessary to price a menu using the stochastic-modeling approach?
    a. Percentage of sales allocated to costs other than food and labor
    b. Raw food cost
    c. Percentage of sales allocated to labor
    d. None of the above

13. Which of the following pricing methods involves the most variables?
    a. The prime cost method
    b. The stochastic method
    c. Non-structured pricing
    d. The factor method

14. Which of the following is vital to menu psychology?
    a. Pricing
    b. The design of menus
    c. How the qualities of menu items are communicated to the customer
    d. All of the above

15. Which of the following is a popular menu strategy in an environment in which restaurants stand to benefit from minimizing the extent to which eating out is associated with the much-lamented obesity epidemic in the United States?
    a. The larger portion option
    b. The smaller portion option
    c. Buffet service
    d. None of the above

16. Which of the following is NOT something to consider when designing a menu?
    a. Item descriptions should not be too long.
    b. A menu should not overuse words not typically associated with food and beverages.
    c. Superlatives such as "cooked to perfection" should always be used.
    d. The description should not state the size of a meat portion unless it is extraordinary.

17. Documentation is not needed if a menu uses which of the following words or symbols representing these words?
    a. Lean/extra-lean
    b. Healthy
    c. Cooked to perfection
    d. Fresh

18. Which of the following is NOT an organization/association that offers reference publications to assist operators in their efforts to understand food-labeling laws?
    a. The Academy of Nutrition and Dietetics
    b. The FDA
    c. The National Restaurant Association
    d. Both b and c

Fill in the Blanks

1. _____ pricing can be adopted more robustly for customers who want items or service styles for which there are few providers or alternatives in the marketplace.

2. _____ is the simplest approach to menu pricing.

3. The _____ is a variation on the factor method and integrates both raw product and labor costs.

4. The _____ is the most common pricing tactic and dates back more than 100 years to hotel-restaurant operators in Europe.

5. The _____ accomplishes the vital goal of including profit in the price of every item on a menu.

6. For the customer, _____ represents discount pricing and convenience; for the operator, it facilitates increased sales.

7. Children's menu items are often considered to be _____—they may not produce a substantial profit but achieve the primary objective of selling food and beverages at profit-producing prices to adults.

8. _____ is the type and number of offerings in each menu category—such as appetizers, entrees, and desserts.

9. _____ is the only pricing method that integrates internal and external variables, including demand functions such as item popularity and market position.

10. _____ includes a broad range of analytical techniques that enable foodservice operators to optimize the menu mix and menu pricing to enhance efficiency, increase guest satisfaction, and maximize profit.

Case in Point: The $47 Burger

Los Angeles, California, is arguably one of the leading destinations for those seeking the quintessential hamburger. California is known as the birthplace of many of today's most-popular drive-through QSR chains, including regional leader In-N-Out Burger. But it is also home to independent QSRs. Tommy, the second-generation owner of one of these independent restaurants, went on a quest to see what was new in the hamburger market.

What he found surprised him. At the time, he was selling a deluxe half-pound cheeseburger topped with chili and onions for $6.95; he thought it was expensive but he had been meticulous in applying advanced menu-pricing approaches and his strategy was paying off—in the last several months it was his best-selling item. The first stop on his quest was the Fleur de Lys, a traditional French restaurant located in Las Vegas's Mandalay Bay Resort and Casino. Here he saw on the menu the FleurBurger—priced at $75! Tommy noted that the burger was unique: It is made of Kobe beef and garnished with foie gras—that's duck or goose liver—and black truffles. While his restaurant does not serve beer or wine, he also noticed that for a mere $5,000 you could get the FleurBurger 5000. This is the same FleurBurger, but it is served with a bottle of Chateau Pétrus 1990 in Ichendorf Brunello stemware, specially imported from Italy, which you take home.

Next, he visited the Old Homestead Steakhouse in Boca Raton, Florida, where he found the tri-beef burger. This is made of a blend of three kinds of beef—American Prime, Japanese Wagyu, and Argentinean. The hamburger is served with its signature chipotle ketchup made with truffles and champagne. The restaurant's owners even donate $10 of every sale of the $125 burger to the Make-A-Wish Foundation.

Thinking he'd found the most expensive burger, he excitedly anticipated a visit to New York City's Wall Street Burger Shoppe. On the menu he found the Richard Nouveau burger—for $175. The ten-ounce Kobe beef burger is topped with black truffles, seared foie gras, aged Gruyere cheese, wild mushrooms, and flakes of gold leaf. But then he heard that Burger King—the same Burger King chain discussed in the previous chapter—had created the world's most expensive hamburger. Served only at the West London Burger King Restaurant, one can pay a whopping $186 for the menu item named simply "The Burger." The Wagyu beef patty is accompanied by white truffles, onion tempura prepared in Cristal champagne, and some of Spain's finest Pata Negra ham. It is presented in an Iranian saffron and truffle bun.

While he was not able to visit London, his explorations had given him much food for thought. He flew back to California and thought to himself, "I could build a burger that, by Los Angeles standards, would be hugely expensive. I could use unique ingredients and charge a nice $46.95— exactly $40 more than my current big seller costs. Would people buy it?"

Should Tommy try it? Would people buy it? What do you think of his pricing approach?

PART III: THE FOODSERVICE OPERATION

Chapter 6: Facilities Planning, Design, and Equipment

Learning Objectives

After becoming familiar with this chapter, you should be able to:
1. Understand the planning considerations that are vital to creating a successful foodservice operation.
2. Appreciate how safety and productivity pertain to facilities planning.
3. Identify the key elements in design and layout, particularly as they pertain to space allocation, dining room design, and kitchen design.
4. Understand what is involved in selecting food preparation and serving equipment.
5. Explain how to procure equipment for a new or remodeled foodservice operation.
6. Utilize practices that lead to enhanced corporate responsibility.

Chapter Outline

- Planning
  - Planning Considerations (Figure 6.1)
    - o Who makes the decisions
    - o Prospectus
    - o A feasibility study
    - o The list of tasks for planning project
  - Safety and Productivity
    - o Safety: food sanitation and safety, safety of the foodservice operation's physical characteristics, guest and employee safety
    - o Productivity: workflow, traffic flow
  - Other concerns
- Design and Layout (Figures 6.2, 6.3)
  - Space Allocation
  - Dining Room Design (Table 6.1)
  - Kitchen Design

- Equipment
    - Equipment Selection
        - Food preparation equipment
        - Serving equipment
    - Equipment Procurement
- Corporate Responsibility
    - Environmental Concerns
    - Energy and Water
    - Building to Reduce Food Waste
- Managerial Implications
- Industry Exemplar: Tutta Bella
- Key Terms
- Case in Point: Trash Cans

Questions for Review

True–False

1. T F Kid-friendly foodservice must not allow space for highchairs.

2. T F An onsite operation in education requires more space than does an operation in correctional foodservice.

3. T F A banquet room in a hotel requires more space than does a fine dining restaurant that offers tableside food preparation.

4. T F The planning phase includes identifying all operational parameters, not just the number of seats in the dining room.

5. T F Even today, almost all foodservice operators follow the traditional rule of thumb whereby they allocate 50 percent of a foodservice operation's space to the dining room, leaving the remaining space to production, a greeting area, restrooms, and so on.

6. T F The key in configuring a dining room's furnishing arrangements is to identify the average group size at a foodservice operation.

7. T F In correctional foodservice, greater separation among individuals in the dining area is not advisable.

8. T F ADA requirements are not very specific, particularly pertaining to wheelchair access.

9. T F Most OSHA violations in the foodservice industry today are due to management error.

10. T F Abiding by legislation that pertains to both guest and employee safety is not a key planning consideration.

11. T F In the planning phase, food sanitation and safety can best be addressed through the layout and selection of kitchen equipment.

12. T F The timeline is critical for coordinating construction and managing costs.

13. T F Information that supports both a prospectus and a feasibility study often comes from the same sources.

14. T F A sound foodservice operation plan should include every conceivable detail about the intended physical and operational characteristics of the foodservice operation, including staffing needs.

Multiple Choice Questions

1. Which of the following comes first in the development of the foodservice operation?
   a. Getting equipment
   b. Planning
   c. Designing
   d. None of the above

2. Which of the following dictates the planning procedures that deserve more attention and time?
   a. The scope of the foodservice operation
   b. The scale of the foodservice operation
   c. Both a and b
   d. None of the above

3. Which of the following comes first in the planning process of developing a foodservice operation?
   a. Identify the decision makers.
   b. Understand the expectations or goals of the planning process.
   c. Ensure that the outcomes address the needs and desires of all stakeholders.
   d. None of the above.

4. Among the following, who makes the decisions in the planning process of developing a foodservice operation?
   a. The owner
   b. The opening general manager
   c. The managerial team
   d. All of the above

5. Which of the following terms refers to the plans that result from the planning process in the development of foodservice operation?
   a. Agenda
   b. Prospectus
   c. Blueprint
   d. None of the above

6. With which of the following should a prospectus begin?
   a. Address the intended customer base.
   b. Create a general description of the foodservice operation.
   c. Determine the operation-specific parameters such as hours of operation and number of seats.
   d. None of the above.

7. Which of the following should be included in a sound foodservice operation plan?
    a. Every conceivable detail about the intended physical and operational characteristics of the foodservice operation, including staffing needs
    b. 20 year pro-forma financial statements
    c. Both a and b
    d. None of the above

8. Which of the following terms refers to the procedure undertaken to determine the resources required to make a foodservice operation a reality?
    a. SWOT analysis
    b. Design process
    c. Feasibility study
    d. None of the above

9. At what stage of foodservice operation development is a feasibility study undertaken?
    a. Prior to developing a prospectus
    b. After developing a prospectus
    c. Both a and b
    d. None of the above

10. Which of the following is a purpose of a feasibility study?
    a. Objectively evaluate the strengths and weaknesses of a proposed business as well as the opportunities and threats in its marketplace.
    b. Determine the resources required to make a foodservice operation a reality.
    c. Calculate the prospects of financial success.
    d. All of the above.

11. Which of the following refers to the function of SWOT analysis?
    a. It objectively evaluates the strengths and weaknesses of the proposed business as well as the opportunities and threats in its marketplace.
    b. It determines the resources required to make a foodservice operation a reality.
    c. It calculates the prospects of financial success.
    d. All of the above.

12. What is the next decision or set of decisions taken after a feasibility study demonstrates that a proposed foodservice operation is financially viable and a detailed prospectus is complete?
    a. Hire employees.
    b. Buy the necessary equipment.
    c. Determine the timeline for the actual construction or remodeling that is needed to create the new operation.
    d. Start off the design phase.

13. In most cases, who determines the timeline for the actual construction or remodeling that is needed to create a new operation?
   a. The project manager
   b. The executive chef
   c. The assistant general manager
   d. None of the above

14. Which of the following is a major component of a timeline?
   a. Timing
   b. Tasks
   c. a and b
   d. None of the above

15. Which of the following is the biggest concern of foodservice operations in terms of guest safety?
   a. Fire hazards
   b. Undergoing loss
   c. Sanitation
   d. None of the above

Fill in the Blanks

1. As is true of any business venture, developing a foodservice operation starts with _____, and this entails determining several basic building blocks.

2. A _____ should begin with a general description of the foodservice operation.

3. The information that supports both a prospectus and a _____ often comes from the same sources.

4. The 1970 _____ Act was created to ensure safe and healthful working conditions by setting and enforcing standards.

5. A properly designed foodservice operation in which _____ has been carefully planned will likely incur lower labor costs by enabling employees to complete their tasks more efficiently.

6. The _____ requires employers to make a reasonable accommodation to any known disability of a qualified applicant or employee.

7. The _____ includes several provisions aimed at making businesses more accessible.

8. A _____ is a drawing or a computer-generated illustration of what a foodservice operation will look like once it is built or remodeled.

9.   Stock equipment is cheaper than _____ that might be necessary to meet special food production requirements, concept requirements, or resolve design and layout issues.

10.   The _____ is a compilation of all the pertinent information related to a particular piece of equipment.

Case in Point: Trash Cans

Julio had worked for many years as a line cook at a series of restaurants, but his eyes were always focused on owning his own. He saw every job he took on as preparation for his eventual real career as a restaurateur.

A few years ago, he started writing down his ideas and potential concepts that might be successful. He soon landed on what seemed like a great idea: A pizza restaurant that specialized in unique combinations and pizza by the slice. He also knew that in the Midwestern college town in which he lived, there was no competition for such a concept.

The day finally came for Julio to quit his day job and start his own business. While he had saved for this venture, his funds were limited and he was intent on building the pizza restaurant, preliminarily named "Julio's Pies," as inexpensively as possible. So, he opted not to hire an architect, attempting to design the place himself. The building he had leased had previously been a furniture store so it was little more than an empty box, which Julio viewed as a benefit, allowing him to create the type of interior that would best fit his concept without having to worry about structural limitations.

His first task was the kitchen. He had learned in his years of cooking that efficient food flow was critical, from receiving to storage to preparation and straight through to delivery to the guest. Looking at his design, he believed that, in spite of his having no professional design experience, his kitchen would be expertly efficient.

He also put considerable time into designing the dining area. The seating was comfortable but not too wasteful in terms of open space and the layout was appropriate for a pizza place. Even in the entry area, the space allowances and relationships were impressive, although it was his first attempt at restaurant design.

Next, he hired a contractor and construction began immediately. The contractor, Bob, had some experience working with drawings and plans created by nonarchitects and, thanks to the simplicity of the design, remodeling the space to create Julio's Pies proceeded quickly. The only glitch was that Bob had made several suggestions to improve the operation, but Julio wouldn't hear of any changes. At one point, Bob even had his wife, Lori, call Julio to appeal to his good sense and make a few modifications. Julio had one word for Lori: "No." He was determined to be the master of his destiny.

So Bob finished the job, for which Julio paid him immediately, and they parted ways. Julio was so excited that he could barely sleep that night. He was already thinking about whether he should open a second unit or franchise the concept.

A few days later, the food began arriving. Almost immediately, Julio realized that he had a problem. He had forgotten all about garbage! There wasn't a single garbage receptacle built into the kitchen or any of the side stations in the dining area. And, because he had created such a compact kitchen, there was no room even for a free-standing trash can.

Remodeling the kitchen would require every dollar he had left, leaving nothing for the initial food orders or payroll.

What advice would you give Julio?
What could he have done to avoid all of this?

Chapter 7: Food Sanitation and Safety

Learning Objectives

After becoming familiar with this chapter, you should be able to:
- Identify the major foodborne illnesses as well as their symptoms and growth conditions.
- Recognize the other hazards that may be present in food and describe their effects.
- Determine how foodborne illness can be prevented.
- Understand how the safety of the work environment is linked to food safety.

Chapter Outline

- Foodborne Illness
    - What are the symptoms?
    - Factors that make controlling foodborne pathogens challenging.
  - What Is Foodborne Illness?
    - Food safety occupies the scientific discipline that studies the handling, preparation, and storage of food to prevent foodborne illness.
    - Pathogens cause foodborne illness:
      - Bacteria (Figure 7.1)
      - Virus
    - Foodservice managers should make it a matter of policy to become familiar with the conditions, which are often referred to as FAT TOM—conditions in which pathogens that cause foodborne illness appear and thrive:
      - Food
      - Acidity
      - Time
      - Temperature
      - Oxygen
      - Moisture
  - US Government Programs
    - Food Net

- Determine the burden of foodborne illness in the United States.
- Monitor trends in occurrences over time.
- Identify specific foods and settings that contribute to specific outbreaks of foodborne illness.
- Develop and assess intervention measures to prevent future occurrences.
  - USDA guidelines should be followed by individual consumers if they suspect they have contracted a foodborne illness:
    - Preserve the evidence.
    - Seek treatment as necessary.
    - Call the local health department.
    - Call the USDA meat and poultry hotline.
- Biological, Chemical, and Physical Hazards in Food
  - Transmission of viruses and parasites
  - Biological contamination
    - Toxins
    - Mercury
    - Physical hazards
  - Bioterrorism
    - The Bioterrorism Act of 2002
- Foodborne Illness Prevention
  - The manager has four primary duties:
    - Identify and use the correct training program.
    - Implement that program with passion, enthusiasm, and determination.
    - Communicate with and listen to employees so that obstacles to correct procedures are removed or corrected.
    - Monitor to reward appropriate behavior and correct unsafe food-handling practices.
  - General Prevention
    - Hand washing

- Guidelines
  - The Hand Washing for Life Institute
  - The Partnership for Food Safety Education
- Sanitization
  - The FDA Food Code for 2010
- Cross-contamination
- Cooking to proper temperature
- Fight Bac! food-handling tips
- The temperature danger zone
- ServSafe

- HACCP
  - Identify and manage the critical control points.
  - Successful implementation depends on having a training routine for safe food handling and preparation.
  - It is important to prevent E. coli contamination.
  - Recalls (see Figure 7.6).

- Workplace Safety
  - When Things Go Wrong Outside the Foodservice Operation
    - Disaster preparation plan
    - Emergency management agencies
    - The US Department of Labor (DOL)
  - Material Safety Data Sheets (Figure 7.7)
    - What are MSDSs? What utility do they offer?

- Managerial Implications

- Industry Exemplar: Microban International

- Case in Point: Food Safety at the Nursing Home

Questions for Review

True False Questions

1. T F Foodborne illness is commonly known as food poisoning.

2. T F Parasites are the most common pathogens that cause foodborne illnesses.

3. T F The most common source of biological contamination is the restroom.

4. T F Cross-contamination occurs whenever a cooked product and a raw product come in contact with each other in any way, including the use of the same utensil for both products.

5. T F The most widely used training programs for all foodservice personnel are NEHA ServSafe.

6. T F Neither the FDA nor the USDA has a website with up-to-date recall information.

7. T F Fire safety and emergency preparedness are not part of foodservice workplace safety.

8. T F In most situations, a foodservice operation is not required to keep a book containing all the Material Safety Data Sheets for every chemical agent used in the facility.

9. T F The first page of any MSD book usually lists emergency numbers that are available 24 hours a day for each company's products.

10. T F Successful implementation of an HACCP program depends on having a training routine in place regarding safe handling and preparation of food and proper sanitation procedures.

Multiple Choice Questions

1. Which of the following make controlling foodborne pathogens challenging?
   a. The global nature of the food supply
   b. The growing preference for food that is prepared and eaten away from home
   c. Improper sanitation practices
   d. All of the above

2. Which of the following is part of food safety?
   a. Handling of food
   b. Storage of food
   c. Preparation of food
   d. All of the above

3. Which of the following is NOT a goal of Food Net?
   a. Determine the burden of foodborne illness in the United States.
   b. Monitor trends in occurrences of foodborne illness over time.
   c. Identify specific foods and settings that contribute to specific outbreaks of foodborne illness.
   d. Educate children in schools about foodborne illness.

4. Which is NOT a guideline according to the USDA but should be followed by individual consumers if they suspect they have contracted a foodborne illness?
   a. Preserve the evidence.
   b. Seek treatment as necessary.
   c. Call the local health department.
   d. None of the above.

5. Which of the following is an example of physical hazard in food?
   a. Mercury in fish
   b. Pesticides
   c. Foreign objects such as glass or metal fragments
   d. All of the above

6. What is the term for the purposeful adulteration or poisoning of food in order to cause widespread illness or death, presumably in service of a political or social cause?
   a. Biohazard
   b. Bioterrorism
   c. Food poisoning
   d. Food hazard

7. Which is NOT a primary duty of the foodservice manager for foodborne illness prevention?
   a. Identify and use the correct training program.
   b. Implement that program with passion, enthusiasm, and determination.
   c. Monitor to reward appropriate behavior and correct unsafe food-handling practices.
   d. None of the above.

8. Which of the following is NOT one of the four simple steps for Safe Food Handling suggested by Fight Bac!?
   a. Clean hands and surfaces often.
   b. Separate, don't cross-contaminate.
   c. Cook—to proper temperatures.
   d. Do not refrigerate promptly.

9. What range of temperature is called the Danger Zone?
    a. Below 32°F
    b. 41°F and 135°F
    c. 0°F and 40°F
    d. Above 135°F

10. What is the name of the book every manufacturer must provide about a product?
    a. Material Safety Data Sheets
    b. Workplace Safety Manual
    c. Sanitation instructions
    d. None of the above

Fill in the Blanks

1. A foodborne illness is commonly known as food _____.

2. The whole purpose of proper food handling is to control the growth of _____.

3. The pathogens that cause foodborne illnesses are _____ organisms, so it is virtually impossible to observe or experience evidence of contamination when it is first introduced.

4. Food should not be in the _____ for more than two hours.

5. The most common source of biological contamination is the _____.

6. _____ is a "heavy metal" that can be harmful to humans as it builds up over time.

7. _____ contamination can cause choking or harm to the digestive system.

8. _____ is the purposeful adulteration or poisoning of food in order to cause widespread illness or death, presumably in service of a political or social cause.

9. According to The FDA Food Code for 2010, _____ means using heat or chemicals to clean food-contact surfaces, that, when tested, exhibit a 99.99 percent reduction in disease microorganisms of public health importance.

10. _____ can occur in many situations but particularly whenever a cooked product and a raw product come in contact with each other in any way, including when the same utensil is used for both products.

11. _____ monitors chemical, biological, and physical food hazards from purchase to service.

12. The HACCP system begins with food producers and processors, all of whom are expected to identify and manage the _____ in that process.

13. The symptoms of the foodborne illness caused by _____ are severe and can include bloody diarrhea, blood problems, kidney failure, and even death.

14. During a _____, all foodservice organizations that have purchased the suspect product should return it for credit to their suppliers.

15. _____ has the overall responsibility for the administration and enforcement of laws enacted to protect the safety and health of workers.

Case in Point—Food Safety at the Nursing Home

Jonathan was known to be an excellent foodservice manager at a large nursing home in a small town in the Midwest. He had run the operation for years and was respected by his employees and his boss. He was active in the community as the coach of a local baseball team. Jonathan succeeded because he made the rules clear. His employees always said: "Jonathan is tough, but you always know what to do. And he'd better not catch you not doing it!" Yes, Jonathan had a tough reputation, and while it meant that no one questioned him, it also meant that the organization had been running smoothly for years. It was almost running itself, he used to say.

A new unit opened in Jonathan's nursing home last year. It was designed to house individuals recovering from serious head and jaw surgery. Often the reconstructive surgery was complicated and the recovery long and patients needed care that could not be provided at home. They couldn't eat regular food, so at first they had to sip liquid food. As they recovered the ability to chew, their food could be ground up. The kitchen had to prepare 10 or 15 servings of ground food. Jonathan's team usually ground the meat after it was cooked and then kept it warm and served it. One day during flu season, several cooks had become ill, and a new cook decided to get some work done for the next day. He ground raw turkey, carefully fried it, and, just as Jonathan had told him to do, he placed it in a nice deep pan and covered it tightly. He was preparing it for the next day and placed it in the refrigerator.

It was served as a ground turkey salad with jellied cranberry sauce garnish the next day for lunch. Starting about 7 P.M. that evening, after the kitchen had closed, patients began to feel nausea and then some experienced diarrhea. By 10 P.M., seven people had become ill, and the nurse called Jonathan at home. His first reaction was, "It's not possible—patients can't have gotten sick in my operation!" By the next day, however, they had isolated the offending organism in the turkey salad and in some biological fluid samples taken from patients.
    1. What happened?
    2. Explain how this outbreak of foodborne illness happened.
    3. What could Jonathan have done to prevent it?
    4. What should he add to his training program in the future?

Chapter 8: Supply Chain Management

Learning Objectives

After becoming familiar with this chapter, you should be able to:
1. Describe the activities in the purchasing process and the role of the purchasing manager.
2. Understand how distribution channels function.
3. Determine how to select suppliers.
4. Explain the importance of ethics, particularly in relation to purchasing.
5. Identify the various methods and related issues pertaining to buying food and beverage products.
6. Appreciate the importance of accurate forecasting.
7. Calculate quantities of food items in various product categories using the most suitable method.

Chapter Outline
- Purchasing

    - Economies of scale are reductions in costs due to efficiencies.

    - Today, managers at both large and small foodservice operations understand that time spent on the purchasing process yields economic and operational benefits that cannot be ignored.

  o Purchasing Activities

    - Determine product specifications.

      - Clear product specifications are critical in standardizing purchasing, food production, and quality.

    - Make-or-buy analysis is both an operational and a financial decision.

    - Decide whether to use locally sourced and locally manufactured foods:

      - Superior freshness

      - Reduction in food miles

      - Reducing associated carbon footprint

  o Purchasing Managers

- In large onsite operations the purchasing function is executed by an entire department that has specialized purchasing managers delineated by product category.Rebates are becoming more commonplace.

- Distribution Channels (Figure 8.2)
  - Foodservice operators use multiple channels of distribution, but the management and profit opportunities are the same.
  - Product Management
    - Explore how products move from the source to the guest
    - Key distribution channel stages:
      - Source
      - Manufacturer or processor
      - Distributor
      - Foodservice operation
      - Foodservice guest
  - Intracompany Distribution Channels
    - Foodservice operators can shorten the supply chain and take on some of the roles traditionally served by manufacturers and processors.Reduce labor requirements at individual restaurants.
    - Reduce cost by eliminating steps in the distribution channel.
  - Profit Maximization
    - In comparing one distributor with another, the operator must take a shopping bag approach in which a wide variety of items are compared.
    - Terms of payment affect profit directly.

- Supplier Selection
  - Selection should not be on the basis of price alone.
  - Supplier as Partner
    - Location
    - The variety of foodservice operations involved
    - Expertise
  - Suppliers and Ethics
    - For a distributor to share or a manager to ask for proprietary information violates professional standards.
    - The manager's personal gain may supplant the benefits to the organization.
    - The ethical treatment of distributors is key.

- Methods of Buying
  - What is centralized purchasing?
  - What is group purchasing?
  - What are group purchasing organizations?
  - What is decentralized purchasing?
  - Who is the prime supplier?
  - How can stockouts be prevented?
  - What is a cost-plus contract?
  - Why would operations use buy and inventory?
- Forecasting
  - What is the needed quantity?
  - Forecasting Models
    - Simple average
    - Moving average
    - Weighted average
    - Modified moving average
    - Exponential smoothing
    - Causal forecasting
  - Calculating Quantities
    - Relatively straightforward, assuming forecasts are accurate and production schedules are prepared accordingly
    - Just-in-case approach
    - Par system
    - Just-in-time (JIT) approach
    - Economic order quantity (EOQ)
  - Unexpected Impacts
- Managerial Implications
- Industry Exemplar: Sysco
- Case in Point: Purchasing in University Dining Services

Questions for Review

True–False Questions

1. T F Supply chain management involves coordinating interconnected businesses that result in a product or service for an end user.

2. T F In the foodservice industry, the supply chain most commonly begins with the customer.

3. T F Economies of scale are reductions in profits due to efficiencies gained as sales volume increases.

4. T F In large onsite foodservice companies the purchasing function is executed by an entire department.

5. T F A distribution channel is the path or pipeline through which goods flow from a vendor to the consumer while payment flows in the opposite direction.

6. T F One of the best ways to understand distribution channels is to explore how products move from the foodservice operation to the guest.

7. T F Supplier selection should always be made on the basis of price alone.

8. T F Purchase quantity = Quantity needed – Quantity on hand

9. T F Causal forecasting uses specific time-series data.

10. T F EOQ determines the point at which the combination of order costs and inventory carrying costs are the least.

Multiple Choice Questions

1. Supply chain management encompasses the planning and management of all activities involved in _____
   a. Sourcing.
   b. Procurement.
   c. Conversion.
   d. Logistics coordination.
   e. All of the above.

2. Purchasing is also referred to as _____
    a. Sourcing.
    b. Procurement.
    c. Conversion.
    d. Logistics coordination.
    e. None of the above.

3. In the foodservice industry purchasing involves _____
    a. Product specifications.
    b. Purchasing specifications.
    c. Determining whether products should be purchased or prepared at the foodservice operation.
    d. All of the above.
    e. None of the above.

4. Which of the following is NOT a stage of a distribution channel in foodservice?
    a. Source
    b. Distributor
    c. Foodservice guest
    d. None of the above

5. In the foodservice industry, distributors do NOT offer which of the following?
    a. Free assistance with menu development
    b. Money-saving alternative food products
    c. Promotional material, nutritional information, or ingredient information
    d. None of the above

6. Which of the following is NOT one of the ways in which food and beverage products are generally distributed to foodservice operators?
    a. By large national or regional distributors with very specialized product lines
    b. By local independent full-line distributors
    c. Through commissary systems, in which food is prepared or portioned prior to distribution to local units
    d. By local independent full-line distributors
    e. None of the above

7. Which of the following is NOT a method of buying used by foodservice operators?
    a. Centralized purchasing
    b. Group purchasing
    c. Decentralized purchasing
    d. Buy and inventory
    e. Purchase and replace

8. What is the name of the process of predicting which food items will be needed for a specific daypart, day, or week?
    a. Procurement
    b. Conversion
    c. Forecasting
    d. Feasibility analysis
    e. Concept mapping

9. Which of the following forecasting approach averages historical data, weighting the most recent data more heavily?
    a. Moving average
    b. Weighted average
    c. Exponential smoothing
    d. Causal forecasting
    e. Modified moving average

10. What is the chief objective in ordering?
    a. Maintaining as much inventory as possible
    b. Maintaining a minimum amount of inventory on hand at all times
    c. Not maintaining any inventory at all
    d. None of the above

Fill in the Blanks

1. Today, managers at both large and small foodservice operations understand that time spent on the _____ process yields economic and operational benefits that cannot be ignored.

2. The first management function of purchasing is determining _____.

3. A _____ is the path or pipeline through which goods flow from a vendor to the consumer while payment flows in the opposite direction.

4. Large distributors frequently host _____ in which foodservice operators can tour the warehouse and learn about new products.

5. _____ are intermediaries who represent processors or manufacturers and deal with assisting purchasing managers.

6. Distributors exhibit varying levels of _____ and amounts of support that they provide to their foodservice clients.

7. In _____, purchasing responsibility and execution is assigned to a department or location that covers multiple foodservice outlets.

8. _____ consists of predicting which food items will be needed for a specific day part, day, or week.

9. The _____ approach averages historical data, weighting the most recent data more heavily.

10. _____ approaches use multivariate statistical models, integrating regression analysis to predict outcomes based on a number of input variables.

11. In many operations where specific items are used routinely, a _____ is used to trigger orders.

12. _____ is essentially an accounting formula that determines the point at which the combination of order costs and inventory carrying costs is lowest.

Case in Point

Carly has just begun working in her new position as the purchasing manager for a large public university's dining services. The university has some 40,000 students spread across its 720-acre campus. In addition to the dining halls in the freshmen dorms, the campus features cafes, coffee kiosks, and convenience stores. Previously, the dining services department did not have a purchasing manager but the general manager hopes that, by instituting this new role, she can save money. In reviewing last year's financial information, Carly notes that last year the university spent some $16 million on food-related products.

Having worked previously with a large restaurant chain, Carly is well aware of the economies of scale that can be achieved in purchasing. She's spent her first week at the new job meeting with distributors' representatives and acquainting herself with the campus. She's a little overwhelmed by the number of vendors, but she knows that she can achieve her boss's main objective, which is to reduce spending on food products without sacrificing quality.

Today, Carly met with the four executive chefs. In essence, the foodservice operation is divided into four quadrants with each including one of the four dining halls and an associated kitchen. Each chef is responsible for food preparation for the respective dining hall and surrounding eateries. Food preparation is completed at each of the kitchens. The chefs have been with the university for many years and work together well. That being said, they operate rather autonomously. The menu at each dining hall is created independently. The belief is that students enjoy the variety of menus and food-preparation styles. Indeed, surveys indicate that the students generally like the food, and the dining services management rarely receives complaints.

Toward the end of the meeting, Carly explores the topic of purchasing. She wants to know why the university uses two national distributors and several local distributors. The chefs explain that they each place orders and that they are satisfied with their distributors, even if they can't agree on using the same vendors.

As she returns to her office, Carly is dismayed that, on any given day, four vendors are on campus delivering the same category of item but each one to a different kitchen. She reviews the invoices from last year, and finds that prices for the same food item vary considerably across vendors while the specifications for the items are the same. She also learns that since each chef uses a small amount of the various products (as compared with the amount used if purchased as a single order) they are not receiving any volume discounts.

What are some changes Carly might consider?

Chapter 9: Food Management

Learning Objectives

After becoming familiar with this chapter, you should be able to:

1. Understand what is essential to the receiving function, including invoice processing.
2. Identify the requirements for proper storage of the full range of food types in various states of preparation.
3. Explain the inventory management function.
4. Determine how to valuate inventory items depending on type of foodservice operation.
5. Apply inventory-turnover analysis.
6. Appreciate the importance of a range of issues pertaining to food production and food quality management.

Chapter Outline

- Receiving

    - The receiver compares the delivered product with the purchase order and the invoice to ensure that they match, and then verifies that the quality, size, and characteristics meet the products' specifications.

    - He then ensures that the price is the same as was quoted when the order was placed.

    - He notifies the kitchen manager or chef about any shortages or missing items and documents any variations between order and delivery.

    - Finally, he begins processing the invoice and delivering the products to their respective storage locations.

    - Barcodes and RFID tags make it easier to keep track of inventory.

  o Receiving Essentials

    - The receiver must know enough about food products that she can discern whether the products coming into her operation meet the specifications by reference to which they were ordered.

    - The receiver must also be trustworthy.

    - Internal control issues make it unadvisable for the receiver to be the person who places orders.

    - Weighing items must be completed before formally accepting delivery.

- The receiving area should consist of or be located adjacent to a dedicated dock that is clean, secure, and convenient for accepting and storing items and transporting them to the kitchen.
  - o Receiving Procedures
    - Confirm that the delivery matches the purchase order.
      - Purchase order summaries are historically referred to as *receiving clerks' daily reports*.
      - In blind receiving, the receiver compares what is delivered with the invoice or with a purchase order that does not contain quantities.
    - Confirm that the invoice matches the purchase order.
      - Compare the purchase order with the invoice.
    - Make accept-or-reject decisions.
      - The receiver must consider recall notices that may pertain to any item received and ensure that these are not accepted.
    - Complete the paperwork.
      - Invoice stamps create a form on the invoice or purchase order where the receiver can indicate the date and other relevant information.
      - Credit memorandum is issued if there is an error in the receiver's favor.
      - The use of barcodes and RFID tags facilitates the automation of receiving, which reduces errors and labor costs associated with managing food in an operation
  - o Invoice Processing
    - Invoice payment schedule
    - Discounts associated with early payment
- Storage Management
  - Stored items must be managed properly to maintain quality, prevent pilferage, and provide for proper use.
  - Security is a vital issue.
    - Dry Storage
      - o Dry goods should be stored between 50°F and 70°F.
      - o Humidity should be maintained between 50 percent and 60 percent, with adequate ventilation.
      - o No direct sunlight should enter a dry storage area.

- Dry storage areas should be safeguarded against rodents, insects, and other pests.

- Items should be arranged to employ a first-in, first out (FIFO) approach.

- Dry storage areas should be segregated from cleaning goods.

- Access to storage areas should be strictly limited to personnel whose job responsibilities require it.

- Refrigerated Storage

  - Refrigerated products should be stored between 32°F and 37°F.

  - Refrigerators may be designated for select product categories that optimally call for slightly different temperatures.

  - Walk-in vs. reach-in refrigerator (see Figures 9.3 and 9.4).

  - Temperatures in refrigerated and frozen areas should be closely monitored.

- Frozen Storage

  - Frozen food should be stored between −10°F and 0°F.

  - The humidity should be high to prevent or reduce moisture loss and freezer burn.

- Inventory Management

  - What is *inventory*?

  - Nonperforming assets produce no revenue until they are sold. (Figure 9.5)

  - Issuing

  - Perpetual Inventory

    - Perpetual inventory systems

  - Physical Inventory

    - Taken weekly, biweekly, or monthly, depending on the nature of the foodservice operation.

    - Inventory audit can minimize or eliminate problems in the physical inventory process.

  - Inventory Valuation

    - Actual purchase price method

    - FIFO method

    - Weighted average price method

- Latest purchase price method
- Last-in-first-out (LIFO) method
  - o Inventory-Turnover Analysis
    - Useful in comparing a single operation over time with a number of very similar operations.
    - This tool is helpful in identifying undesirable trends in inventory valuation.

- Production Management
  - The last step in food management prior to delivery to the guests is preparing the food to be served.
  - o Production Procedures
    - The first step in food production is forecasting production needs.
      - Overproduction
      - Underproduction
    - Production sheet formats vary based on type of operation (Figure 9.9).
    - Production meetings provide opportunities to discuss current and upcoming issues.
  - o Managing Food Quality
    - Establish quality standards.
    - Train employees.
    - Select correct production equipment.
  - o Quantity Food Production
    - Portion control
      - First, a foodservice manager must determine what size per portion is desired.
      - Next, the chosen portion sizes must be communicated clearly to all relevant staff as a component of the operation's quality standards.
      - The third step is to measure items, which could require a portion scale or measuring utensils.
      - Finally, portion control must be monitored.

- Managerial Implications
- Industry Exemplar: CBORD
- Case in Point: The Automotive Plant

Questions for Review

True–False Questions

1. T F Dry storage items should be held at temperatures between 50° F and 70° F.

2. T F Temperatures in refrigerated and frozen areas should be closely monitored.

3. T F It is acceptable to refreeze thawed frozen food.

4. T F In the foodservice industry, inventory refers to all food and beverage products on hand.

5. T F Inventory management is the process used to requisition items from storage for kitchen areas or units in an onsite foodservice operation.

6. T F In the perpetual inventory system a running record of which products are on hand is kept.

7. T F Food cost = Beginning inventory + Food purchased – Ending inventory.

8. T F The value of each item in an inventory must be calculated in order to determine the cost of goods used during a given period.

9. T F The first step in food production is forecasting production needs.

10. T F Portion control in food production ensures that serving sizes are uniform.

Multiple Choice Questions

1. Stored items must be managed properly to:
   a. Maintain quality
   b. Prevent pilferage
   c. Provide for proper use
   d. All of the above

2. The typical range of humidity for dry storage is:
   a. 0–10 %
   b. 30–40%
   c. 70–80%
   d. 50–60%

3. In dry storage, items should be arranged according to _____
    a. LIFO.
    b. FIFO.
    c. It doesn't matter; any approach is fine.
    d. None of the above.

4. Refrigerated storage should typically maintain temperatures between:
    a. 0–10°F.
    b. 20–30°F.
    c. Below 32°F.
    d. 32–37°F.

5. Humidity in a freezer unit should be high to prevent or reduce which of the following?
    a. Freezer burn
    b. Moisture loss
    c. Both a and b
    d. None of the above

6. Items that produce no revenue until they are sold are called _____
    a. Performing assets
    b. Profit-maximizing assets
    c. Nonperforming assets
    d. None of the above

7. Proper inventory management can do which of the following?
    a. Reduce costs.
    b. Increase operational efficiency.
    c. Lead to greater guest and employee satisfaction.
    d. All of the above.

8. In the perpetual inventory system, the inventory is updated in real time through integration with which of the following?
    a. Point-of-sale terminals
    b. Requisition orders
    c. Invoices
    d. All of the above

9. Which of the following is NOT an inventory valuation method?
    a. Actual purchase price method
    b. FIFO method
    c. Moving average method
    d. Weighted average price method
    e. Latest purchase price method

10. Which of the following is NOT a step in the receiving process?
    a. Confirm that the invoice matches the purchase order.
    b. Confirm that the delivery matches the purchase order.
    c. Make accept-or-reject decisions.
    d. Complete the paperwork.
    e. None of the above.

Fill in the Blanks

1.   Most products delivered by large distributors are packaged with _____.

2.   _____ result in fewer readability issues than barcodes do and can be read remotely, often at a distance of several yards.

3.   The receiver's most important tool is a _____.

4.   During delivery confirmation, food items are weighed and inspected for quality based on _____.

5.   Some foodservice managers prefer _____ to labor-intensive confirmation steps.

6.   In the event that something listed on an invoice was not received—it wasn't included in the delivery, it was rejected, or the price is overstated on the invoice due to an error—the delivery person will issue a _____.

7.   Humidity for dry goods should be maintained within a range of between 50 and 60 percent, with adequate _____.

8.   The adoption of _____ works best when all products regardless of storage area are dated at the time of purchase.

9.   The humidity in a freezer unit should be high to prevent or reduce _____.

10. _____ is the process used to requisition items from storage for kitchen areas or units in an onsite foodservice operation.

11. _____ systems were once considered too labor-intensive for large foodservice operations.

12. The _____ is a valuable tool that can minimize or eliminate potential problems in the physical inventory process.

13. _____ practice is rarely advisable as it can artificially inflate food costs for a given period and can lead to apparent fluctuations in month-to-month comparisons.

Case in Point: The Automotive Plant

Recently, Chen joined the management team that operates the foodservice operation at an auto-manufacturing plant in the southeastern United States. The foodservice is available 24 hours per day, seven days per week. (The plant runs three eight-hour shifts per day.) On average, they serve about 4,500 meals per day. As the general manager, Chen oversees a team of seven managers and 57 employees.

During the hiring process, the plant's administration made it clear to Chen that their business is assembling cars—not foodservice management. Still, they assured him that they want to provide quality food to their employees; they just prefer not to be bothered with operating what they consider a support service. That's why he'd be hired. Moreover, they don't want to lose money—they can't afford to subsidize the foodservice operation even as a benefit to employees. Thus, their directions to Chen were simple: Manage the foodservice such that high-quality hot food is available 24 hours a day—and don't lose money doing it!

Chen's first order of business, then, was to wrap his arms around the financials. He knew the labor cost would be higher than in some operations owing to the 24-hour-a-day operation. He also knew that, given the volume of food served, inventory management would be an important element in his success.

Chen was immediately struck by the incredible amount of food stacked and piled up in the various storage areas. It was not very orderly. The meat refrigerator, for example, had three areas in which hamburger meat was stored. He also noted that nothing was dated.

He met with the production manager, John, to discuss inventory issues. John explained to Chen that receiving staff were just too busy to date items when they arrived. He added that, since the volume of foodservice was so high, it would be almost impossible for food to go bad. As for the abundance of food, John said that he'd been managing the kitchen for 15 years and until now no one had complained about inventory levels.

Not particularly pleased with John's responses, Chen decided first to check the accuracy of the operation's inventory valuations. In this way, he could perhaps better help John to improve the situation. He performed an inventory audit of the major meat items and found that the amounts listed on the inventory sheets far exceeded the amounts that were on hand. He also learned that the prices listed for items had not been updated, which artificially lessened the resulting food cost determinations.

Chen sat at his desk wondering about his next steps. Obviously, someone was inaccurately recording the amount of food on hand. In addition, why weren't the prices updated?

What steps should Chen take next?

PART IV: GENERAL MANAGEMENT

Chapter 10: Financial Management

Learning Objectives

After becoming familiar with this chapter, you should be able to:
1. Describe what generates foodservice sales and understand why we need to apply accounting principles.
2. Understand the components of income statements, balance sheets, and cash flow statements.
3. Apply analytic tools to the various financial statements.
4. Explain the various cost concepts as they apply to foodservice operations.
5. Appreciate the importance and nuances involved in creating a budget and describe what is involved in budgeting for capital improvements.

Chapter Outline

- Accounting Overview
    - Restaurant Industry Dollars
        - Sales generators (Figure 10.1)
        - Expenses by category (Figure 10.2)
    - Unique Industry Aspects
        - Common variables to all foodservice operations
        - Consumer behavior and the interrelationship between hospitality and general business practices
        - Supply chain management
        - Labor intensiveness of foodservice operations
    - Accounting Principles
        - Uniform system of accounts
        - Established accounting principles
            - Cost principle
            - Business entity

- Consistency
- Financial Statements
    - Income Statement (Figure 10.6)
        - Varies slightly from segment to segment
        - Sales
        - Cost of sales
        - Gross profit
        - Operating expenses
            - Direct vs. indirect
            - Depreciation
            - General and administrative expenses
            - Other expenses
            - Interest
    - Balance Sheet (Figure 10.7)
        - Assets
            - Current
            - Fixed
            - Other
        - Liabilities
            - Short-term
            - Long-term
        - Shareholders' equity
    - Statement of Cash Flows (Figures 10.8, 10.9)
        - Cash flow from operating activities
        - Cash flow from investing activities
        - Cash flow from financing activities
        - Preparation: Direct vs. indirect method
- Analyzing Financial Statements
        - Compiling them and ensuring their accuracy

- - Using the information to identify problem areas, make operating decisions, and plan for the future
  - o Income Statement Analysis
    - Consider each of these categories separately
    - Variance analysis (Figure 10.10)
  - o Operating Ratio Analysis
    - Average check
    - Seat turnover
    - Sales per seat
    - Food cost and beverage cost
    - Cost of goods sold
    - Labor cost
    - Prime cost
  - o Balance Sheet Analysis
    - Liquidity
      - Current ratio
      - Accounts receivable turnover
      - Acid test ratio
    - Solvency
      - Solvency ratio
      - Debt-equity ratio
    - Asset management
      - Fixed asset turnover
      - Asset turnover ratio
    - Profitability
      - Profit margin
      - Operating efficiency ratio
      - Return on assets
- Cost Concepts

- - Understand the types of expenses that foodservice managers must manage.
  - Fixed versus Variable Costs
    - Semifixed or semivariable
  - Controllable vs. uncontrollable costs
  - Overhead
- Budgeting
  - Advantages
    - Serves as a goal with quantified objectives
    - Serves as a benchmark of operating performance
    - Assigns responsibility appropriately
    - Can help an operation cope with foreseeable adverse situations
  - Disadvantages
    - Creating a budget, especially for a new restaurant or onsite foodservice operation, requires a considerable investment in time.
    - It is based on forecasts, which may not be accurate.
    - In a chain or managed-services setting, a budget is effective only if it is supported by the overarching organization.
    - A budget that is created in a corporate headquarters and simply given to a particular unit without consideration of the operation's particular situation, market, or location may be wildly inaccurate.
    - Budgeting requires full disclosure about all areas of an operation.
  - Operations Budget
    - Most common in foodservice management
    - Approaches
      - Incremental budgeting
      - Zero-based budgeting
  - Capital Budget (Figure 10.12)

- The net present value (NPV)
- The time value of money
- Internal rate of return (IRR)
- Managerial Implications
- Industry Exemplar: Pullman Regional Hospital
- Case in Point: You Can't Take Percentages to the Bank

Questions for Review

True–False Questions

1. T F Fixed asset turnover is an asset management ratio.

2. T F Solvency ratios are generally used to assess a foodservice operation's ability to meet its short-term financial obligations.

3. T F In foodservice operations, the indirect method of preparing a statement of cash flows is better than the direct method.

4. T F Cash flows from financing activities include cash inflows from investors (including banks and shareholders).

5. T F Foodservice operations typically have less than 5 percent of their total assets invested in food.

6. T F Income statements do not vary at all from segment to segment.

7. T F Seat turnover ratio indicates how many guests per daypat use a given seat.

8. T F Operating efficiency ratio is a type of solvency ratio.

9. T F Overhead is a controllable cost.

10. T F In zero-based budgeting, a manager does not rely on historical data at all but forecasts, calculates, and justifies every revenue and expense item.

Multiple Choice Questions

1. Which statement provides a summary of an operation's profit (or loss) for a given period?
   a. Balance sheet
   b. Statement of cash flows
   c. Income statement
   d. The company's bank statement

2. Depreciation is listed under which of the following categories in an income statement?
   a. Cost of sales
   b. Operating expenses
   c. Fixed assets
   d. None of the above

3. Which of the following tangible capital or fixed assets is not taken into account under depreciation?
   a. Buildings
   b. Machinery
   c. Land
   d. None of the above

4. Which of the following sections is NOT found in a statement of cash flows?
   a. Cash flows from financing activities
   b. Shareholder's equity
   c. Cash flows from investing activities
   d. None of the above

5. What is the name of the process of comparing actual with budgeted figures in income statement analysis?
   a. Variance analysis
   b. Average check
   c. Accept-or-reject decisions
   d. None of the above

6. Which of the following is not a liquidity ratio?
   a. Current ratio
   b. Acid test ratio
   c. Accounts receivable turnover
   d. Debt-equity ratio

7. Which of the following are considered the capstone of financial ratios?
   a. Solvency ratios
   b. Profitability ratios
   c. Liquidity ratios
   d. Asset-management ratios

8. Which of the following is NOT a characteristic of an operations budget?
   a. Its timeframe is typically a month.
   b. It is formatted using the sales and cost categories.
   c. It includes percentages.
   d. None of the above.

9. Which of the following is NOT one of the most appropriate capital budgeting methods for the foodservice industry?
   a. Internal rate of return
   b. Net present value
   c. Payback period
   d. None of the above

10. Which types of costs change in direct proportion to sales?
    a. Variable costs
    b. Fixed costs
    c. Both a and b
    d. None of the above

Fill in the Blanks

1. The _____ provides a summary of an operation's profit (or loss) for a given period, which is typically calculated on a weekly or monthly basis.

2. _____ comprise expenses other than the basic food and beverage expenses that are addressed in an income statement.

3. The _____ presents a summary of a foodservice operation's financial condition at a given point in time.

4. _____ can be prepared using either of two methods: the direct method or the indirect method.

5. A high current ratio will likely lead an operator to assess the _____.

6. The _____, sometimes referred to as the revenue and expense budget, is the most common in foodservice management.

7. _____, such as monthly rent or management salaries, do not change, no matter whether a foodservice operation is very busy or very slow.

8. The _____ is the present value of cash flows minus the investment that makes those cash flows possible.

9. Determining a realistic discount rate depends on accurately calculating the _____.

10. _____ is a useful ratio for quickly assessing how well the major cost categories in any foodservice operation are being managed.

11. _____ ratios measure the extent of debt financing that a foodservice operation has assumed and serve as partial indicators of the operation's ability to meet these long-term obligations.

Case in Point: You Can't Take Percentages to the Bank

Carl had worked hard in his several years of foodservice management. He lacked a college degree, but he had prevailed in the competitive industry by using common sense and an appreciation of how people, namely one's employees, can make the difference between success and failure. He also took the time to read industry trade magazines.

So, when he got the call from Mutual Insurance's corporate headquarters to run its sizable cafe, he knew he was ready. The first few days on the job were spent getting to know the employees, the facility, and the customers. He was excited and confident that he was in the right position at the right time. Following this brief orientation, he was scheduled for a meeting that would set the parameters of his mission.

When he met with his new boss, the vice president of human resources, he immediately noted that the tone was very different from the upbeat, cheerful attitude that Carl had encountered during his interviews. Today, Candace Sherman was all business. Candace started by explaining to Carl that his predecessor was asked to leave Mutual Insurance because of the losses the cafe had incurred. The food was excellent, the foodservice staff was relatively happy, and the customers were generally pleased with the food, but the man Carl had replaced had not managed the costs well. Candace added, "Your predecessor was a very nice person, but for the six months he worked here he ignored my requests for a financial report. He kept telling me that he had all the numbers in his head and that the operation was profitable so there was no need for concern. He said that food cost and labor cost were each under 40 percent, so he knew he was profitable. When we were audited last month, we learned that he was losing about $10,000 a month. This is why he was fired. We can't afford to lose money anymore. That is why we hired you, owing to your many years in the business."

Carl wasn't sure what to say. On the one hand, it sounded like he was receiving a compliment, but on the other it sounded like a warning. Until today, he had no idea what had happened to the previous manager.

After an unpleasantly long silence, Candace leaned forward over her desk and looked Carl straight in the eye. "By Friday, I expect a comprehensive budget for the foodservice operation. I will hold you to the budget, and while I don't expect the cafe to make a ton of money, I expect the realistic profit shown on your budget to be achieved."

With that, the meeting was over. Carl went back to his small office and found that the drawers were empty. There were no financial records of any kind. There wasn't even a calculator. It was then that Carl began to panic. He had never created a budget, and while he knew that controlling expenses was important, he'd never been asked to consider the financial side of the business.

If you were worked for Carl, how would you help him?

Chapter 11: Customer Service

Learning Objectives

After becoming familiar with this chapter, you should be able to:

1. Identify several examples of customer service philosophy and explain what they mean to a foodservice organization.
2. Identify factors that should be measured to identify problems and successes.
3. Review quality control and quality maintenance issues and understand how to set standards of quality performance.
4. Identify service failures and apply service recovery techniques.

Chapter Outline

- Style and Philosophy
    - Developing a customer service mentality
    - Description of any foodservice operation
    - Harvey's "Crash Course on Customer Service"
  - Customer Service Experience
    - Disney as a benchmark of excellence in customer service
    - Guestology
  - Exceeding Expectations
    - Five dimensions of quality customer care
      - Reliability
      - Responsiveness
      - The Feeling of Being Valued
      - Empathy
      - Competency
    - Quint Studer's use of the concept of hardwiring
      - Rounding for results
    - Fred Lee's application of the Disney philosophy to healthcare
      - Most significant themes for teaching patient-focused care
        - Sense people's needs before they ask.

- o Help each other meet those needs.
- o Acknowledge people's feelings.
- o Respect everyone's dignity and privacy.
- o Explain what's happening.
- Measurement
  - ▪ Immediate feedback from customers themselves
  - ▪ Obtaining data
  - o Problem Identification
    - ▪ Comment cards or other such feedback channels
    - ▪ Mystery shoppers
    - ▪ Use of technology
      - Recorded customer phone calls
      - Self-administered guest surveys
      - Second-generation web services
      - Online dining reservation websites
    - ▪ Gathering feedback in hospitals
      - Making rounds
      - Survey
      - Data reliability
      - Data validity
      - Comparing with other hospitals
      - Assigning scores
  - o Data Management
    - ▪ Importance of measuring customer perception
    - ▪ Maintaining accurate records
    - ▪ Careful investigation of customer complaints
- Quality and Standards
  - ▪ Service standards
    - Disney's example (Figure 11.4)
      - o Safety
      - o Courtesy

- o Show
- o Efficiency
  - Rank Orders of Customer Priorities (Figure 11.5)
    - o The good food standard
    - o The friendliness standard
    - o Communication
    - o Empathy
  - Understanding performance benchmarks
- o Success
  - If a foodservice operation achieves outstanding performance benchmarks, how does that translate into success as a business?
  - How does it build a customer base of people who return, again and again, to the same restaurant or facility?
    - Loyalty
    - Moments of truth
- Service Failure and Recovery
  - Every failure is a valuable opportunity.
- o Service Recovery Strategies
  - Service recovery theme
    - o ACT:
      - Acknowledge and apologize with no excuses.
      - Correct the issue/make it right.
      - Take action or take it forward.
    - o GIFT:
      - Give a sincere apology.
      - Inform the customer.
      - Fix the problem.
      - Thank the customer.
    - o RELATE:
      - Recognize the problem.
      - Empathize with the customer.

- Listen closely and pay attention.
- Apologize.
- Take action to correct the problem.
- Explain.
  ○ The "A" Team:
    - Awareness of the problem.
    - Acknowledge the mistake.
    - Apologize; listen actively.
    - Act to amend.
○ Results
    - Employees must therefore be empowered to make decisions about how and when to make amends.
    - Turn a lost customer into a loyal customer.
- Managerial Implications
- Industry Exemplar: Starbucks
- Case In Point: Pineapple or Pickle—Who's to Say?

Questions for Review

True–False Questions

1. T F Reliability is the strength of the conclusions or inferences associated with data collected from surveys.

2. T F Employees should be empowered to make decisions about how and when to compensate a customer for a problem, for example by providing a free dessert as part of service recovery.

3. T F American Airline's performance record has consistently been recognized as one of the benchmarks of excellence in customer service.

4. T F It is not common for every department in a large organization to have a standard service recovery gift.

5. T F At Disney, customers are constantly invited to complete face-to-face surveys in the parks.

6. T F Research from the Center for Hospitality Research at Cornell University suggests that many disgruntled patrons save their complaints for later, making it hard for an operator to correct real or perceived wrongs.

7. T F A hospital normally seeks feedback from its patients regarding only its food.

8. T F Service recovery is an opportunity to turn a lost customer into a loyal customer.

9. T F The whole purpose of standards is to ensure that the quality experience a foodservice operation communicates is actually experienced by the customer.

10. T F In case of a service failure, an operation needs, in addition to a plan, a *service recovery theme*.

Multiple Choice Questions

1. What term does Disney use for market and customer research?
   a. Guestology
   b. Customerology
   c. Guestofication
   d. None of the above

2. Which of the following is not one of the five dimensions of quality customer care?
   a. Reliability
   b. Responsiveness
   c. Perseverance
   d. A feeling of being valued.
   e. Empathy

3. Which of the following is the most sought-after measurement of customer opinion?
   a. Customer tipping behavior
   b. Immediate feedback from customers themselves
   c. Customers' body language
   d. Customers' repeat behavior
   e. None of the above

4. Which of the following is the name of the activity undertaken to address mistakes, failures, and misfortunes in a foodservice operation?
   a. Service restoration
   b. Service recovery
   c. Operation failure
   d. Service failure
   e. None of the above

5. Which of the following is a disadvantage of using a mystery shopper service to gather customer feedback?
   a. The feedback is delayed
   b. The feedback is costly
   c. Both a and b
   d. None of the above

6. Which of the following is not an example of "the good food standard"?
   a. Serving temperatures
   b. The quality of serviceware
   c. The menu setup
   d. Eye contact

7. Which of the following is not one of the ways in which Disney is undertaking market and customer research?
   a. Customers are constantly invited to complete face-to-face surveys in the parks.
   b. "Listening posts" are created at specific locations to answer questions, solve problems, and collect information.
   c. Comment cards are everywhere, and cast members throughout the parks collect the opinions and observations of guests as part of their jobs.
   d. When entering and leaving the park, it is mandatory for customers to participate in a short interview session.

8. On which of the following have restaurants and onsite foodservice operators traditionally relied for problem identification?
    a. Internet reviews
    b. Phone calls to customers
    c. Comment cards or other such feedback channels
    d. None of the above

9. Which of the following is NOT a technology-intensive way in which customers can provide immediate, live feedback?
    a. Recorded customer phone calls
    b. The use of mystery shoppers
    c. Self-administered guest surveys
    d. Second-generation web services
    e. Online dining reservation websites.

10. Which of the following is not one of the four dimensions of the service standard of Disney?
    a. Efficiency
    b. Show
    c. Safety
    d. Courtesy
    e. None of the above

Fill in the Blanks

1. Disney's performance record has consistently been recognized as one of the _____ of excellence in customer service.

2. _____ can be the most important dimension of quality customer service, and often the most lacking.

3. By far, the most sought-after measurement of customer opinion is _____ from customers themselves.

4. Traditionally, restaurants and onsite foodservice operators have relied to a considerable extent on _____ or other such feedback channels.

5. Today, _____ provides many opportunities for customers to provide immediate, live feedback.

6. _____ depends on using a survey tool that produces consistent results.

7. In the foodservice business, all that matters is customer _____.

8. A _____ is when the customer experiences something that leads to a change in his opinion or impression.

9. Activity undertaken to address mistakes, failures, or misfortunes is called _____.

10. Most operations want to reduce _____, sometimes specifying a certain number per quarter by which to reduce their overall total.

11. _____ must be empowered to make decisions about how and when to make amends.

Case In Point: Pineapple or Pickle—Who's to Say?

Jake is a foodservice director at a 500-bed university hospital. He is a registered dietitian with a master's degree in business administration. He has 20 years of experience, having worked his way up from pot washer to waiter to chef's assistant. After college, he chose to work in the healthcare segment and ultimately he landed his dream job, for which he is very well qualified. Jake deals with customer service issues every day. On this particular day, he is told by one of the foodservice workers that a patient in room 715 is irate and has already called administration to register a complaint. As Jake glances at his phone, he sees a text message from his boss regarding this incident. Jake is very busy today—there are five major catering events requiring his attention, an employee disciplinary panel to attend, the monthly budget analysis is due, and he was hoping to leave early to catch his son's soccer match. The associate tells Jake that the patient would not really tell her what the problem was—she just kept mumbling something about rotten food.

Jake immediately tells his catering manager to proceed with the first event without him and heads up to the seventh floor, dreading the confrontation he knows is coming. He checks in with the nurse who is responsible for this patient. She tells him the patient is very ill and very upset about her illness. He knocks on the door of room 715, asks if he can come in, and, upon entering, introduces himself as the foodservice director. He sees a middle-aged woman, very pale and thin, with several IV lines in both arms—Mrs. Martin. She does not look at him, but says, "How on earth can you serve rotten food to sick people in a hospital?" Jake pauses a moment, and then says how sorry he is that something was wrong with her food. He adds that he will just need a bit more information to be sure he can correct the problem. He also quickly adds that any error in this hospital's foodservice delivery is unacceptable to him because he knows how difficult it is to be sick and in the hospital. "Rest assured," he notes, "I will personally guarantee your future meals are problem-free. Now, can you tell me what happened?"

Mrs. Martin frowns, but finally makes eye contact with Jake, who has moved to a point by her bed where she can easily see him. She says that she loves pineapple, but when she took a big bite of this morning's pineapple, it was rotten. (Now Jake knows that the pineapple came in fresh yesterday and he himself had some for breakfast in the hospital cafe. There have been no other complaints.)

How does Jake handle the rest of this situation, and what is your prediction about the outcome?

Chapter 12: Marketing

Learning Objectives

After becoming familiar with this chapter, you should be able to:
1. Define marketing, understand that there is a scientific basis for marketing, and discuss some of the major approaches.
2. Discuss the implications associated with social marketing.
3. List the concepts involved in and understand the value of strategic marketing to foodservice operations in all sectors.
4. Understand how marketing works within an organization and across key segments of the foodservice industry.

Chapter Outline

- Science of Marketing
    - Marketing involves two types of research: primary and secondary.
- Social Marketing
    - Following today's successful marketing approaches, foodservice operations can:
        - Reduce the amount of, or the impact of, their waste byproducts on the environment.
        - Stress their healthy, nutritious food, thus appealing to the current health-conscious customer.
        - Offer locally or organically produced foods.
        - Build energy efficiency into their production areas, dining areas, etc.
    - Trends in social marketing reflect being socially responsible and increased diversity.
- Strategic Marketing
    - Strategic marketing helps an organization do the following things:
        - Position itself against its rivals.
        - Anticipate changes in demand and technology and adjust accordingly.
        - Influence the nature of the competition by changing the market.
    - Competitive Forces

- Porter's five forces of strategic marketing apply to all areas of business (Figures 12.1, 12.2).
- The normal curve is bell-shaped (Figure 12.4).
- The long tail occurs when customer satisfaction is distributed more thinly along a broad range (Figure 12.5).
- Sticky ideas are simple, unexpected, concrete, credible, and emotional.
    - Marketing Mix
        - Marketing mix consists of product, price, place, and promotion (the four P's).
        - Marketing plan is an outline of how the marketing will take place.
- Service Marketing
    - The customer-service gap is the difference between what customers expect and what they receive.
- Marketing and Unit-Level Operations
    - Text Your Papa
    - The Test of Taste
    - Onsite Foodservice Marketing
        - A healthcare foodservice operation must develop a very careful strategy to combat brown-bagging.
- Branding
    - Branding Basics
        - National concepts
        - Regional concepts
        - Signature concepts
        - Manufacturer's brands
    - Keys to Successful Implementation
        - Umbrella branding
- Managerial Implications
- Industry Exemplar: Freshëns
- Key Terms
- Case in Point: The Entrepreneurial Baker
- Review and Discussion Questions

Questions for Review

True False Questions

1. T F Marketing and customer service must be coordinated to give the customer what he wants.

2. T F The science of marketing does not lay the foundation for strategic decision-making.

3. T F Advertising a foodservice organization's offering of locally or organically produced foods is a socially oriented marketing approach.

4. T F Quality often drives customer preferences or judgments of product value more directly than does cost alone.

5. T F The best approach to formulating strategy begins with a clear objective or end goal.

6. T F The relative weights of Porter's competitive forces do not vary by industry.

7. T F The "new economics of culture and commerce" of the editor-in-chief of *Wired* magazine, Chris Anderson, is based on "the long tail."

8. T F The marketing plan must align with the foodservice operation's core values and operating objectives.

9. T F Marketing a service is not different from marketing a product.

10. T F The intangible aspects of the foodservice business are not important to consider in the context of service marketing.

11. T F The size of the customer-service gap corresponds to the degree of dissatisfaction.

12. T F In onsite operations, marketing within your own company, healthcare facility, or school system becomes your major focus.

13. T F Onsite operations do not accept text messages or e-mails for pre-ordering of menu items from their dining facilities.

14. T F Healthcare facilities always run multiple foodservice units.

15. T F Healthcare foodservice marketing never emphasizes grab-and-go eating.

Multiple Choice Questions

1. What is the main focus of marketing activities?
   a. The employees.
   b. The vendors.
   c. The customer.
   d. The board of directors of the organization.

2. According to John Lawn in the February 2010 issue of the trade journal *Food Management*, which of the following foodservice operations must be featured in order to achieve high participation rates and customer satisfaction?
    a. Characteristics that appeal to a broad mix of demographic, cultural, and age groups.
    b. Workforce diversity.
    c. Competition among related firms.
    d. None of the above.

3. In what type of marketing research is a problem or question identified, a study designed and conducted, and data compiled and analyzed?
    a. Primary research.
    b. Secondary research.
    c. Tertiary research.
    d. None of the above.

4. What type of marketing research involves gathering data from existing sources to characterize the status of the current market or competition?
    a. Primary research.
    b. Secondary research.
    c. Tertiary research.
    d. None of the above.

5. Which is a growing trend in foodservice that reflects a social marketing orientation?
    a. Advertising to selected demographics.
    b. Emphasizing value.
    c. Emphasizing quality.
    d. Advertising contributions to environmental and health issues.

6. Strategic marketing helps an organization do which of the following things?
    a. Position itself against its rivals.
    b. Anticipate changes in demand and technology and adjust accordingly.
    c. Influence the nature of the competition by changing the market.
    d. All of the above.
    e. None of the above.

7. Which of the following is not one of Porter's Five Forces?
    a. Threat of new competition.
    b. Bargaining power of suppliers.
    c. Rivalry with competition.
    d. Position of organization in the business lifecycle.
    e. Bargaining power of buyers.

8. Which of the following is a characteristic of a sticky idea?
   a. It is unexpected.
   b. It is concrete.
   c. It is credible.
   d. It is emotional.
   e. All of the above.

9. Which of the following is NOT a characteristic of a sticky idea?
   a. It is complex.
   b. There is at least one story that ties all of these properties together.
   c. It is credible.
   d. It is emotional.
   e. None of the above.

10. What is the primary step in any strategic marketing approach?
    a. Creating the appropriate marketing mix.
    b. Clearly defining the target market.
    c. Gathering customer feedback.
    d. None of the above.

11. What is the secondary step in any strategic marketing approach?
    a. Creating the appropriate marketing mix.
    b. Clearly defining the target market.
    c. Gathering customer feedback.
    d. None of the above.

12. What is the most important step in any strategic marketing approach?
    a. Creating the appropriate marketing mix.
    b. Clearly defining the target market.
    c. Both a. and b.
    d. None of the above.

13. Which concept refers to the combination of elements that a foodservice manager manipulates to maximize business?
    a. Marketing mix.
    b. Mission statement.
    c. Marketing theme.
    d. None of the above.

14. Which of the following is NOT included in a marketing mix?
    a. Product.
    b. Place.
    c. Price.
    d. Plan.
    e. None of the above.

15. Which of the following is the product in any foodservice operation?
    a. Only the food.
    b. Only the service.
    c. The overall dining experience.
    d. None of the above.

Fill in the Blanks

1. _____ and customer service must be coordinated to give the customer what he wants.

2. _____ often drives customer preferences or judgments of product value more directly than cost alone does.

3. A marketing mix consists of a specific configuration of product, price, place, and _____.

4. A _____ is an outline of how marketing will take place.

5. The _____ gap is the difference between the service that customers expect and the service that they actually receive.

6. In foodservice, _____ is the inclusion of brand-name products or concepts into the menu or product mix.

7. _____ brands are most commonly used to accent a relatively standard menu item by giving it added market appeal.

8. Lately, healthcare foodservice marketing emphasizes both grab-and-go eating as well as a _____ concept.

9. A healthcare foodservice operation must develop a very careful _____ to combat brown bagging.

10. Those engaging in _____ marketing must try to anticipate customer preferences along with potential customer peculiarities.

Case in Point: The Entrepreneurial Baker

Carole has always loved carrot cake. Even as a teenager, she began to bake her own, always tweaking the recipe, making subtle changes to the ingredients. She became particularly interested in achieving not only the perfect taste but also the healthy properties of carrot cake. She carefully selected oil with more "omega-3's" and healthy sweeteners to augment the nutritional value of carrots. She often enlisted her friends to taste her experiments, and finally, in her last two years of high school, she actually began a small business—she was considered *the* source of birthday cakes for most students in her school. There was no doubt that Carole would become a pastry chef, and that she did.

After attaining her culinary school diploma, Carole's intent was to operate her own business. The catch was, there were many bakeries in the large city in which she lived, and a lot of them featured very well trained pastry chefs with high-profile reputations. They were turning out great cakes in all kinds of shapes and decorations. The competition was fierce. Carol found a very small storefront, which had housed a bakery that had gone out of business. It had most of the equipment she needed. She also had a friend who would be able to assist her in obtaining the smaller pieces of equipment she needed. What she did not have was a plan.

1. Help Carol develop a marketing plan by devising a slogan she can use to market her bakery.
2. What are the major issues Carole will have to consider in developing her marketing plan?
3. What should be the major focus of Carole's strategy?
4. Be creative . . . describe what you think Carole's shop might look like.
5. Carole has her carrot cake, but can she stay in business on carrot cake alone? Suggest some additional products Carole might add and explain why they fit her mission.
6. Suggest some names for Carole's store.

Chapter 13: Human Resource Management

Learning Objectives

After becoming familiar with this chapter, you should be able to:
1. Write and interpret a job analysis and job description.
2. Identify the basic techniques of employee recruitment, selection, and retention.
3. Understand the principles of and methods that apply to scheduling and staffing.
4. Appreciate the applicable laws and processes involved in determining compensation.

Chapter Outline

- What Is the Job?
    - What "the right job" involves
  - Job Analysis
    - Job analaysis is often conducted with the assistance of a job analyst consultant.
    - Job analysis typically involves conducting interviews, administering questionnaires, observing employees on the job, monitoring work logs, and so on.
  - Job Description (Figure 13.1)
    - What is included?
    - Job specification
    - Performance standards (Figure 13.2)
- Finding, Hiring, and Keeping the Best People
  - Recruitment
    - Finding and hiring the right people for the right jobs is a never-ending challenge.
    - "Hire for Attitude, Train for Skills."
    - Design an effective job application.
  - Selection
    - Good interviewing follows a useful framework.
      - The behavioral interview
      - Panel interviews
      - Peer interviews
  - Retention

- How does the organization keep an employee on the job?
- Reducing turnover
- Rewarding and recognizing a "job well done"
- Stay interview
- 360-degree feedback for performance assessment
- Using exit interviews to determine whether there's a fixable cause of turnover

  o Training and Development

  - Professional development
  - Training model (Figure 13.3)
  - Empowerment

- Staffing and Scheduling

  o Staffing and scheduling are often planned together, but they are not the same process.

  o Full-time equivalent or FTE employees can be calculated.

  o Use employee scheduling software.

  o Use a timebar (Figure 13.5).

- Compensation

  o Compensation requires a system for managing everything you have agreed to give to your employees in exchange for their labor.

  o Laws regulate compensation:

  - The Fair Labor Standards Act (FSLA)
  - The McNamara-O'Hara Service Contract Act (SCA)
  - Walsh-Healy Public Contracts Act (PCA)
  - The Immigration and Nationality Act (INA)
  - The Family and Medical Leave Act (FMLA)
  - The Consumer Credit Protection Act (CCPA)
  - Equal Employment Opportunity laws (EEO)
  - Common areas of wage and hour violations in foodservice operations
  - The Taft-Hartley Act

- Managerial Implications

- Industry Exemplar: Morrison

- Case in Point: New Employees or New Motivational Techniques?

Questions for Review

True False Questions

1. T F Empowered employees do not have to check with supervisors at every minor decision point.

2. T F Effective training can be excellent motivation for employees.

3. T F The advantages of 360-degree feedback performance assessment include the sense on the part of the employee that her performance evaluation is not one-sided or biased by personal animus.

4. T F Most organizations suggest conducting 120-day reviews for newly hired employees.

5. T F Panel interviews can empower employees and increase employee satisfaction.

6. T F It is important that a behavioral interview consist of a series of yes/no questions.

7. T F Today's foodservice organizations are looking for diversity.

8. T F Traditionally, foodservice managers have looked for employees with prior experience in a specific industry segment—restaurants, hospitals, schools, etc.

9. T F A mismanaged recognition program can lower morale, especially if criteria are not clear and favoritism is suspected.

10. T F Performance standards allow managers to evaluate job performance with a high degree of objectivity.

11. T F Exit interviews do not provide managers with an opportunity to identify and correct trouble spots in an organization.

12. T F Staffing is not based on job analysis.

13. T F In almost all areas of the foodservice industry, a day lasts longer than eight hours.

14. T F Compensation is highly regulated, with rules governing overtime pay, holidays, shift differentials, and other factors.

15. T F Equal Employment Opportunity laws (EEO) protect employees from being discharged by employers because their wages have been garnished over a single debt.

16. T F Tips may not be pooled with management personnel or other staff who do not usually receive them.

17. T F Organizations large enough to attract the interest of applicable unions usually do not keep legal counsel on staff and do not provide HRM support to the foodservice manager.

Multiple Choice Questions

1. Which of the following do most organizations conduct for newly hired employees?
   a. 30-day reviews.
   b. 90-day reviews.
   c. 360-day reviews
   d. Both a and b.
   e. None of the above

2. Which of the following is not true regarding a 360-degree feedback performance assessment?
   a. It can be time consuming and difficult to administer.
   b. A worker receives feedback from only one source.
   c. Poorly implemented 360-degree evaluations cause resentment and distrust.
   d. None of the above.

3. In a 360-degree process, a worker can receive feedback from which of the following sources?
   a. Peers.
   b. Subordinates.
   c. Customers.
   d. Suppliers.
   e. All of the above.

4. Which of the following is an excellent method for asking questions that allow potential employers and employees to evaluate each other?
   a. Behavioral interview.
   b. Panel interview.
   c. Peer interview.
   d. None of the above.

5. Which of the following is an advantage of peer interviews?
   a. Provides employee satisfaction.
   b. Reduces turnover.
   c. Empowers employees.
   d. All of the above.
   e. None of the above.

6. Which of the following is NOT an example of a circumstance or behavior that provides grounds for terminating an employee immediately?
   a. Theft.
   b. Coming late to work once in a while.
   c. Unexcused absence (no call, no show).
   d. Serious sanitary code violations.

7. Which of the following is a possible way to achieve some organizational benefit when good people leave an organization?
   a. Stay interviews.
   b. Exit interviews.
   c. Panel interviews.
   d. Peer interviews.

8. Which of the following can be a reason for training a veteran employee?
   a. Teaching the right way to do something.
   b. Correcting a behavior that needs improvement.
   c. Instituting a new standard or method of complying with a regulation.
   d. All of the above.
   e. None of the above.

9. Which of the following do many organizations employ to manage complex scheduling situations?
   a. Full-time equivalent or FTE employees.
   b. Performance standards.
   c. Division of labor.
   d. None of the above.

10. Which of the following is incorporated as compensation in some foodservice organizations?
    a. Free liquor at the bar.
    b. Meals.
    c. Free groceries.
    d. None of the above.

11. Which of the following entitles eligible employees to take up to 12 weeks of unpaid, job-protected leave for certain family and medical reasons?
    a. The Family and Medical Leave Act (FMLA).
    b. Immigration and Nationality Act (INA).
    c. Consumer Credit Protection Act.
    d. None of the above.

12. Which of the following is NOT one of the most common areas of wage and hour violations in restaurants, according to Schneider?
    a. The failure to pay overtime for all hours worked.
    b. Improper application of tip credits.
    c. Misclassification of individuals as exempt from overtime.
    d. The failure to maintain records chronicling either hours of work or application of tip credits.
    e. Hiring illegal workers and paying them off the record.

13. Which of the following does a compensation package NOT normally include?
    a. Health care.
    b. Vision care.
    c. Dental care.
    d. A retirement package.
    e. Auto insurance.

14. What is the most common way of notifying employees about their shifts in a restaurant?
    a. Informing them every time in person.
    b. Sending out regular e-mails.
    c. Displaying a schedule in a timebar.
    d. None of the above.

15. Which of the following is NOT part of Southwest's recruitment and retention program?
    a. Hiring people who have failed in the past.
    b. Giving yourself the freedom to be yourself.
    c. Training for skill, but hiring for spirit, spunk, and enthusiasm.
    d. Defining your own standard of professionalism.

16. Which of the following prohibit specific types of employment discrimination on the basis of race, color, religion, sex, age, national origin, or status as an individual with a disability or a protected veteran?
    a. The Family and Medical Leave Act (FMLA)
    b. Immigration and Nationality Act (INA)
    c. Consumer Credit Protection Act
    d. Equal Employment Opportunity laws (EEO)
    e. None of the above

17. Scheduling software usually does not require the user to plug in which of the following:
    a. Number of employees.
    b. The weekend coverage pattern.
    c. Opening and closing hours.
    d. Salary of the employees.

18. Which of the following specifies very clear rules regulating what employers can do, balancing the powers of labor and management?
    a. The Family and Medical Leave Act (FMLA).
    b. Immigration and Nationality Act (INA).
    c. Consumer Credit Protection Act.
    d. Equal Employment Opportunity laws (EEO).
    e. None of the above.

Fill in the Blanks

1. Writing an accurate, effective job description begins with _____.

2. _____ specify the functions or roles involved in particular positions and list the specific responsibilities or tasks to be performed.

3. A _____ describes the conditions, minimum skills needed, and educational or training qualifications associated with a job.

4. The _____ is a non-profit group that supports diversity in the food and hospitality industry, focusing on leadership development as well as employment.

5. The first step in recruiting the "right people" is designing an effective _____.

6. _____ interview questions ask applicants to give specific examples of how they have performed in the face of a problem in the past.

7. In the _____ interview process, a variety of individuals interview candidates using standardized interview questions.

8. One of the newer methods for conducting performance assessment is known as _____.

9. When good people leave an organization, it is possible to achieve some organizational benefit using _____ to determine whether there's a fixable cause of the turnover.

10. The final aspect of retention is training, which for managers is often termed _____.

11. The _____ entitles eligible employees up to 12 weeks of unpaid, job-protected leave for certain family and medical reasons.

Case In Point: New Employees or New Motivational Techniques?

Johanna was furious. She has been the foodservice manager for a 500-student middle school for the past 15 years. She remembers how she felt when she was first hired as a cafeteria line person in a school in her hometown, 25 years ago. She was so excited to have the job and she had always wanted to work with kids. Since she also loved food and wanted to go on to college, this would be a job she loved and one that could help her earn money for college. She loved her job. Or, as she often pointed out, she loved most of her job. The kids didn't always like the food, and they could sometimes be "difficult," but since Johanna was close to their age, she was often the one they came to with complaints. In the beginning, she would pass them on to her supervisor, who usually said there was no money, or the equipment was old, and nothing changed. Johanna eventually stopped passing these comments on and vowed she would run things differently. So why is she furious today?

She can't remember when it happened, but one day she noticed that her employees no longer seemed to care. The cafeteria line was messy, the lines repeatedly ran short on food, workers never smiled at kids, and, worst of all, they frequently called in sick. She hated Mondays because she was always having to work at least two jobs in addition to her own. She wished she had some way to catch these people out having fun when they had called in sick. It happened again today and for her, it was the last straw. She went to see the school district's HRM director and told her story. "Why," she complained, "can't we get the right people these days? I would have loved to have one of these jobs. You have got to find me some good people . . ."

Leon, the HRM director, compared Johanna's departmental turnover numbers with those of other school departments and compared them with those of other middle schools in the district. Her turnover rate was much higher and complaints about the food were increasing. This made Johanna even more furious and she told Leon she might quit. Leon said that was not the solution. He said he could help her design a plan "to find her employees doing something *right*." Johanna heard that phrase and something in it reminded her of something she learned in school. She calmed down and told Leon she wanted to try.

1. You are now Leon. List the things you are going to ask Johanna to do.
2. What skills do you think Johanna may have stopped using over the years?
3. What can she remember from her days as an employee to help her?
4. List some resources Johanna may want to use.

Chapter 14: Leadership and Management

Learning Objectives

After becoming familiar with this chapter, you should be able to:
1. Describe how our conception of leadership has evolved over the last 100 years.
2. Understand the difference between leadership and management as well as the behaviors and functions each entails.
3. Identify the key principles that lead to effective supervision.
4. Appreciate the importance of ethics in foodservice management, and explain the ethical dimensions of customer and employee relations.

Chapter Outline

- Leadership's Evolution
  - Leadership Theories
    - Behavioral theories
    - Types of leadership: Lewin studies, Ohio State studies, and Michigan studies
    - The managerial grid (Figure 14.1)
    - Path-goal theory (Figure 14.2)
    - Contingency theory
  - The Leader of Tomorrow
    - New tasks for future leaders proposed by Peter Drucker
    - Substitutes for leadership raised by Kerr and Jermier (Table 14.1)
    - Servant leadership
- Leadership versus Management
  - Similarities and Differences (Table 14.2)
  - Leadership Behaviors
    - Ten behaviors are suggested by the transformational and servant leadership theories.
    - Skills are needed to behave consistently for the ten principles.
  - Management Functions

- Planning
- Organizing
- Directing
- Controlling

- Supervision
  - The Differences between managers and supervisors
    - Technical skills
    - Interpersonal skills
    - Conceptual skills
  - 12 supervision principles

- Leadership Development
- Ethics
  - Ethics and the Guest
  - Ethical Treatment of Employees
    - Sexual Harassment
    - Pay and Promotion Discrimination

- Managerial Implications
- Industry Exemplar: Jack's Oyster House
- Case in Point: Daphne's Dilemma

Questions for Review

True False Questions

1. T F Transformational leaders are focused on an organization's needs and goals and achieve these through charisma.

2. T F Technical skills are more important for managers or leaders than they are for supervisors because managers or leaders must understand very clearly how to perform the tasks that their employees perform.

3. T F In the course of succession planning, a foodservice organization must identify its short- and long-term management needs.

4. T F Interpersonal skills are the most important skills for managers.

5. T F Early philosophies of leadership did not focus exclusively on characteristics and competencies.

6. T F Conceptual skills in today's environment include understanding the political, social, and economic forces that might affect a foodservice operation.

7. T F The Situational Leadership Model focuses on the readiness of subordinates as the primary conditional situation.

8. T F According to the managerial grid theory, the organization-man manager emphasizes production and efficiency, largely by minimizing the need for interpersonal contact.

9. T F In the Ohio studies on leadership theory, consideration is leader behavior aimed at nurturing collaborative workplace relationships.

10. T F The Lewin studies suggest that a leader's behavioral style changes based on external factors such as situation or setting.

Multiple Choice Questions

1. Which characteristic belongs to the democratic style of leadership?
   a. Being inclusive.
   b. Being directive.
   c. Being controlling.
   d. None of the above.

2. Which study of leadership theory defines a leader's behavior based on how she creates the emotional atmosphere in the workplace?
   a. The Ohio study.
   b. The Lewin study.
   c. The Michigan study.
   d. None of the above.

3. Which of the following is one of the two dimensions of the Managerial Grid?
   a. Concern for people.
   b. Concern for production.
   c. Concern for self.
   d. Both a. and b.
   e. None of the above.

4. Which of the following is NOT one of the five key styles of leadership according to the managerial grid theory?
   a. The team manager.
   b. The impoverished manager.
   c. The country club manager.
   d. The philosophical manager.
   e. The authority-obedience manager.

5. Which of the following is NOT one of the three dimensions of favorableness according to Fiedler's contingency theory?
   a. Task structure.
   b. Position power.
   c. Leader-member relations.
   d. None of the above.

6. Which of the following is NOT one of the four leadership behavioral styles according to the path goal theory?
   a. The directive style.
   b. The supportive style.
   c. The achievement-oriented style.
   d. The laissez-fair style.
   e. None of the above.

7. Which of the following is the primary contention of Leader-Member Exchange (LMX) theory?
   a. The fit between a leader's preferred style and the favorableness of a situation dictates a foodservice operation's effectiveness and success.
   b. Leaders do not treat all subordinates alike.
   c. The leader's primary role is clearing a path so that employees can reach the goal.
   d. A leader's behavioral style does not change based on external factors such as situation or setting.

8. What is the newest evolutionary stage of the leader of tomorrow?
   a. Servant leadership.
   b. Transformational leadership.
   c. Transactional leadership.
   d. None of the above.

9. Which of the following belongs to succession planning?
   a. Identifying what skills and knowledge are needed to be a successful manager.
   b. Creating training programs or providing formal education.
   c. Both a. and b.
   d. None of the above.

10. Which of the following is NOT one of the questions in Blanchard and Peale's ethics check for managers?
   a. Is it legal?
   b. Is it balanced?
   c. How will it make me feel about myself?
   d. None of the above.

Fill in the Blanks

1. The _____ theories attempted to separate leaders from other members of an organization based on physical attributes, personality characteristics, and even appearance or age.

2. The _____ studies suggested that a leader's behavioral style does not change based on external factors such as situation or setting.

3. The _____ manager focuses almost exclusively on the needs of employees and interpersonal relationships within the workplace but focuses little time and energy on the quality or quantity of departmental output.

4. The _____ theory posits that the fit between a leader's preferred style and the favorableness of a situation dictates a foodservice operation's effectiveness and success.

5. _____ involve the ability to interact and communicate with others.

6. _____ in the foodservice industry can be defined as unwelcome sexual advances, requests for sexual favors, or other verbal or physical conduct of a sexual nature.

7. _____ discrimination is a problem of particular concern in the foodservice industry because of the large numbers of women and minorities in employee ranks.

8. The _____ effect is referred to as organizational bias in the workplace that prevents minorities and women from advancing to leadership positions.

9.   To work with able but unwilling employees, those at the third level on the maturity scale, the leader needs to use a _____ style, which combines high relationship concern with low task concern.

10. Mature employees accept _____, relieving a leader of concern for both the task and the relationship.

Case in Point: Daphne's Dilemma

Daphne had an outstanding internship with a managed-services company while she was in college. It allowed her to shadow the medical center's management dietitian and observe the leadership and management skills that made her successful. So, when Daphne earned her registered dietitian credentials, she was thrilled that the same managed services company made her an offer to be the clinical dietitian at Holy Family Hospital. That was five years ago.

Since then, Daphne has honed her skills well and is now considered one of the better managers in the company. She communicates well, delegates when appropriate, and most find her to be very likable. Her manager, Joan, who has run the foodservice department, has been hugely successful in her 25 years on the job. She has also served as Daphne's mentor. Now the time has come for Joan to retire, in two months. She plans to move to her country cottage and enjoy her leisure time with the grandkids.

Today, Joan has suggested that Daphne consider two positions that are open in the company. The first and the one that Joan is clearly urging Daphne to take is the one she, Joan, is about to vacate. The other position is good, too. It is at a medical center of similar size but is in a nicer part of town and, according to all accounts, is in a better position financially. There has been a lot of turnover at the other hospital and the last foodservice director was just fired; he'd been there for only six months. The salary, which would be a nice increase from what Daphne currently earns, would be the same at either location.

Daphne is thrilled to be considered for this promotion, but truly doesn't know what to do. She tends to obsess over such decisions and this one is no exception. She spent hours last night drafting a list of the advantages and disadvantages (of which she can think of very few) corresponding to each location. Then, she remembered a table that she had seen in one of her college textbooks. She can't remember exactly, but recalls that it pertained to selecting jobs with differing criteria. After a short search of her shelves, she finds the book and with little effort finds the table (see Table 14.3). She smiles that she used her favorite highlighter on the title, indicating that this was something she needed to remember.

	Strong Predecessor	Weak Predecessor
Inside Successor	Chances unfavorable	Chances uncertain
Outside Successor	Chances moderately favorable	Chances very favorable

Chances of Success in Various Types of Managerial Succession

1. If you were Daphne, what would you list as positives for staying at Holy Family? What are the negatives?
2. Make the same list for the other opportunity.
3. What would you do?

Part V: Advanced Management

Chapter 15: Internal Control

Learning Objectives

After becoming familiar with this chapter, you should be able to:

1. Explain why internal controls are necessary and why they are particularly important in the foodservice industry.
2. Describe the conditions that lead to employee theft.
3. Understand the general principles of internal control.
4. Appreciate the various ways in which employee theft can be identified.
5. Identify how employees can themselves serve as the best deterrents to employee theft.

Chapter Outline

- Why Is Internal Control Necessary?
  - Foodservice Characteristics
    - Foodservice is still primarily a cash business.
    - All products used are consumable or easily usable by the average person.
    - Contract foodservice providers had excellent internal controls for cash and food.
  - Employee Characteristics
    - Most line positions are relatively low-skilled jobs and relatively low in pay and social status.
    - Most lineworkers are trained on the job.
    - Often lack a strong sense of loyalty to an operation.
    - People with experience at one foodservice operation can usually find a similar job at another.
- Conditions Conducive to Fraud and Embezzlement
  - Opportunity
    - Opportunity is the one condition over which management has the greatest influence.
    - It is the foundation of internal control.

- Need
  - Personal financial struggles can drive an honest person to steal.
  - Addiction may also drive an employee to steal.
  - It is hard for managers to anticipate this condition of fraud or embezzlement.
- Failure of Conscience
- General Principles
  - Divide Duties
  - Fix Responsibility
  - Limit Access
  - Minimize Cash Banks
  - Minimize Inventory
  - Conduct Random Audits
  - Maintain Accurate Records
  - Routinely Upgrade Firewalls and PCI Standards
  - Rotate Managers
  - Keep the Customer in Mind
- Identifying Employee Theft
  - What to Watch For
    - Auditing cash registers
    - Watching for cash and credit-card tips
  - Mystery Shoppers
    - Mystery shoppers help a foodservice operation improve customer relations and indicating breaches of internal control.
    - Friends and family members can be invited to serve as mystery shoppers.
    - Some companies create their own mystery shopping services.
  - Trust
    - Foodservice managers must trust their instincts.
    - The most important way to build trust is to treat employees ethically and with respect.
  - Technology

- More and more foodservice operations are integrating closed-circuit television (CCTV) systems.
- CCTV allows managers to see much more from a single position.
- CCTV can help managers observe employee behavior.
- The Best Deterrent
  o Internal control works best when employees have integrity.
  o Internal control practices must be included in the training process.
  o Employee theft is often contagious.
- Managerial Implications
- Industry Exemplar: A. H., Inc.
- Case in Point: Pennies, Nickels, and Dimes

Questions for Review

True False Questions

1. T F In many segments, foodservice is still primarily a cash business.

2. T F The primary purpose of internal control is to safeguard the assets of a business against losses that result from error or fraud.

3. T F Most electronic cash registers and POS systems now feature a single cash drawer for a single terminal.

4. T F An operation should not change all its locks whenever managers are replaced.

5. T F Drop safes allow for deposits but not withdrawals by employees.

6. T F Requiring cashiers to count out large sums of money is highly inefficient since it consumes a lot of time.

7. T F Inventory on hand should be kept as high as possible.

8. T F It is not a good practice to rotate managers for duties such as counting inventory.

9. T F Foodservice operations increasingly are integrating closed-circuit television (CCTV) systems to monitor cash handling.

10. T F Mystery shoppers help a foodservice operation improve customer relations.

Multiple Choice Questions

1. According to a National Restaurant Association estimate, about what percent of a foodservice operation's inventory losses results from employee theft?
    a. 50%
    b. 100%
    c. 75%
    d. 25%
    e. None of the above

2. Which of the following is a general principle that, if followed thoughtfully and consistently, minimizes the likelihood of employee theft and fraud?
    a. Limit access.
    b. Divide duties.
    c. Fix responsibility.
    d. Minimize cash banks.
    e. All of the above.

3. Which of the following is NOT a general principle that, if followed thoughtfully and consistently, minimizes the likelihood of employee theft and fraud?
    a. Conduct random audits.
    b. Maximize inventory.
    c. Maintain accurate records.
    d. Routinely upgrade firewalls and PCI standards.
    e. None of the above.

4. What is the name of the practice that requires the receiver to compare what is delivered with an invoice or with a purchase order that displays no quantities?
    a. Double count.
    b. Blind receiving.
    c. Internal audit.
    d. None of the above.

5. Which of the following ensures that an operation is charged only for what was delivered?
    a. Double count.
    b. Blind receiving.
    c. Internal audit.
    d. None of the above.

6. What is the name of the practice that involves adjusting the amount of a gratuity slightly so that the last digit equals the sum of the digits to the left of the decimal point of the total check and gratuity amount?
    a. Gratuity adjustment.
    b. Checksum.
    c. Check audit.
    d. None of the above.

7. Which of the following should managers watch for to identify employee theft?
    a. Variances in sales.
    b. Financial ratios and advanced analytic techniques.
    c. Dramatic changes or unexplained patterns in inventory-turnover-analysis data.
    d. Auditing cash registers and looking at cash and credit card tips.
    e. All of the above.

8. Which of the following are most affected by the practice on the part of foodservers of altering tip amounts or adding tips when none was indicated by the customer?
    a. Business travelers.
    b. Leisure travelers.
    c. Local guests.
    d. None of the above.

9. Which of the following is the best deterrent to theft, fraud, or error in a foodservice operation?
   a. Mystery shoppers.
   b. Effective internal control.
   c. Its employees.
   d. None of the above.

10. Which of the following is a role of mystery shoppers in foodservice?
    a. Helping a foodservice operation improve customer relations.
    b. Helping foodservice operations by indicating breaches of internal control.
    c. Both a. and b.
    d. None of the above.

11. How can foodservice operations use mystery shoppers?
    a. Outsource the service to third parties.
    b. Use their own employees as mystery shoppers.
    c. Invite friends and family members to serve as mystery shoppers.
    d. All of the above.

12. Against which of the following must management weigh the benefits of internal control?
    a. The financial costs.
    b. Potential compromises in customer service.
    c. Both a. and b.
    d. None of the above.

13. Which of the following is a benefit to internal control of rotating managers in a foodservice operation?
    a. Foodservice operations can hire fewer managers as every manager becomes experienced in every department.
    b. It increases the chances of stealing/fraud.
    c. More people take an interest in important operational concerns and more people share the labor involved in applying internal controls.
    d. All of the above.

14. Why is it important to protect data and records with firewalls or virus scanners in a foodservice operation?
    a. To safeguard customers' credit card information.
    b. So that customer information is not used for marketing purposes.
    c. To prevent hacking.
    d. All of the above.

Fill in the Blanks

1. The most important enabling condition for theft in foodservice operations is _____.

2. _____ data security standards, which specify credit card processing procedures, must be routinely upgraded.

3. _____ requires the receiver to compare what is delivered with an invoice or with a purchase order that displays no quantities.

4. Dramatic changes or unexplained patterns in _____ data are good indicators that something is wrong.

5. _____ involves adjusting the gratuity amount slightly so that the last digit equals the sum of the digits to the left of the decimal point of the total check and gratuity amount.

6. More and more foodservice operations are integrating _____ systems to monitor cash handling.

7. The principle of maintaining accurate records lies at the foundation of _____.

8. Larger companies are creating their own _____ services rather than outsourcing.

Case in Point: Pennies, Nickels, and Dimes

Bridget had the best job in the world—she managed one of the most popular nightclubs in New Orleans. There was a line to get in every night, the club was profitable, and the owners were pleased with her performance. Moreover, she had a great staff with almost no turnover. Why would anyone not want to work at Stubblefield's?

Stubblefield's featured two levels, an upper story with pool tables, air hockey, electronic darts, and several large television screens. Food was also served on the upper floor. Offerings included the usual bar fare but its chicken wings were by far the most popular items and included variations such as Sweet and Spicy, Asian, and Atom Bomb—the hottest one.

The lower floor was designed around a large dance floor. There were two separate bars; the larger of the two was staffed by two bartenders while the smaller was designed for one bartender and was used primarily on Friday and Saturday nights. Typically, there were three or four cocktail servers, with up to five on busy nights. Opposite the two bars was the DJ booth. On a slow Monday night, the head bartender, John, was scheduled for his break at 11:00 p.m. However, Bridget was trying to finish her annual performance reviews and wanted to complete Katie's review when her shift ended at 11. So, Bridget went behind the bar around 10:30 and asked John if he would mind taking his break then, rather than waiting. Bridget was puzzled by

John's hesitation; she couldn't figure out what difference it would make if he took his break a little earlier. After a moment, John left to go to the employee break room.

Bridget hadn't been a full-time bartender since college, but she could still cover for her employees (so long as it wasn't too busy). Mondays weren't usually very busy, so she had no qualms. She looked around and noticed that everything was clean. John had obviously been using the idle time provided by the slow night well. Just then, a customer ordered a draft beer. Bridget served the guest and made change from John's register. She noticed that three nickels were in the pennies slot in the register. It struck her oddly because John was her best bartender and was meticulous about money handling. He was never over or short when it came time to count the money in his register at the end of the night.

On a whim, Bridget got a reading from the register for cash sales for the night using her code key. (Only managers could generate such information.) She found that the drawer had an excess of $15. She thought it odd, but figured it must be a mistake.

At the end of John's shift, he counted the money in his cash drawer while seated in the manager's office, which was the practice for every bartender. Bridget casually sat at her desk, which was positioned across from where John was sitting. She then accessed the total sales for John's shift on her computer. He submitted the exact amount that was due.

What happened to the $15? Given that John was her best bartender and very proud of his cash handling, Bridget just let it go.

On another Monday night a few weeks later, Bridget decided that, while she trusted John, the prior event deserved attention. So, around 9 p.m., she asked John to take a break for a quick inventory in the beer storeroom. As John commonly did this (but usually before his shift) when it was time to place an order, John thought nothing of the request and promptly left the bar. Bridget immediately checked the cash sales and then opened the cash drawer. This time, there was a quarter in the penny slot and three pennies on top of the quarters. Bridget did a quick cash count and found the drawer had an excess of $28. Yet when John finished his shift, his cash deposit was exactly correct.

Is there something wrong here? What should Bridget do?

Chapter 16: Operational Analyses

Learning Objectives

After becoming familiar with this chapter, you should be able to:

1. Describe how revenue management can be applied to foodservice operations and explain the interrelationship of sales, expenses, and profit.
2. Apply a range of cost analysis techniques, which ultimately lead to more effective pricing.
3. Explain how operational productivity is quantified and how such assessment differs by segment.
4. Understand the Pareto principle, identify management functions to which it applies, and understand the alternative strategies for carrying out these functions that it suggests.

Chapter Outline

- Revenue Management
  - Revenue Management in Restaurants
    - Revenue management is the right seat in the right place to the right customer.
      - Implement a series of concepts each of which uniquely corresponds to a given segment in every market.
      - Marketing: Communicate the value proposition to potential customers.
    - The right price
      - Prices can be manipulated in order to maximize revenue.
      - Pricing applications include happy hour specials during low-demand periods and late-night appetizer discounts.
      - Offer discount coupons and premium pricing.
      - Specialty menus (see Figure 16.1).
    - The right duration
      - Streamline the efficiency with which food is prepared and served.
  - Break-Even Analysis

- Break-even point (BEP) (see Figure 16.2).
  - Address costs with both fixed and variable components accordingly.
- Contribution margin is the contribution to profit resulting from revenue less variable expenses.
  - Contribution rate = (Profit + Fixed costs)/Total sales
- Price Elasticity
- Cost-Analysis Techniques
  - Activity-based Costing
    - ABC allows us to view fixed expenses as a direct function of a foodservice operation.
    - Four distinct cost drivers:
      - Direct cost drivers
      - Batch cost drivers
      - Product-level cost drivers
      - Facility-sustaining cost drivers
  - Potential Food Cost
    - Potential versus actual food cost.
    - Justification for this approach is related to forecasting difficulties, the perishability of food, and the inescapable fact that any type of food production nearly always results in at least a small amount of waste.
    - Current advances in food tracking, the availability of preportioned items, and greater culinary expertise have largely eliminated the need for this practice.
- Operational Analysis Techniques
  - Partial-Factor Productivity Analysis
    - Sales per labor hour
    - Meals per labor hour
    - Equivalent meal value (EMV)
    - Shortcomings
    - Intertemporal analysis

- Floating equivalent-meal-price factor (EMP)
  - Total-Factor Productivity Analysis
    - Two critical measures of quality in foodservice: customer satisfaction and employee satisfaction
- Pareto Principle
- Managerial Implications
- Industry Exemplar: Benihana
- Case in Point: Sales and Labor

Questions for Review

True False Questions

1. T F Companies implementing revenue management effectively report up to 20% greater revenue than do those that forgo such techniques.

2. T F Foodservice operators approach revenue management in the same way that related industries such as airlines or hotels do.

3. T F Every foodservice manager hopes to generate elastic demand for her menu offerings.

4. T F In markets where many restaurants compete for market share, demand is elastic.

5. T F The basic industrial model defines productivity as input divided by output.

6. T F Under the Pareto Principle, foodservice managers should identify the 20% of employees, customers, or issues that require 80% of their time.

7. T F Partial-factor productivity analyses are not good indicators of overall performance since they serve only as measures of isolated aspects of an operation.

8. T F In total-factor productivity analysis, quality measures are not simply integrated as variables in a ratio statistic but instead are integrated into highly sophisticated computer models.

9. T F The application of partial-factor productivity analysis is limited in fine dining.

10. T F Activity-based costing allows managers to trace fixed costs to individual menu items.

Multiple Choice Questions

1. Which are expenses that increase whenever a specific food item is prepared?
    a. Direct cost drivers.
    b. Product-level cost drivers.
    c. Batch cost drivers.
    d. Facility-sustaining cost drivers.
    e. None of the above.

2. Which of the following is NOT an advantage of activity-based costing?
    a. Makes it possible to allocate all expenses.
    b. Allows for identification and reduction of activities that cost more than they add in value.
    c. Is subjective in terms of cost allocation
    d. None of the above

3. What is the name given to the cost of food under perfect or ideal conditions?
   a. Ideal food cost.
   b. Potential food cost.
   c. Future food cost.
   d. Perfect food cost.
   e. None of the above.

4. What is the name of the concept that refers to the effective use of resources to achieve operational goals?
   a. Adequacy.
   b. Productivity.
   c. Profitability.
   d. Break-even analysis.
   e. None of the above.

5. In which of the following is the partial-factor statistic NOT useful?
   a. Fine dining restaurants.
   b. Midscale and theme restaurants.
   c. Quick service restaurants.
   d. None of the above.

6. In the corrections, education, and healthcare onsite foodservice segments, what is a common partial-factor productivity measure?
   a. Meals per labor hour.
   b. Seat turnover.
   c. Number of customers per hour.
   d. None of the above.

7. Which of the following that is NOT an operational issue that separates B&I operations from their traditional-restaurant brethren makes the sales-per-labor-hour measure less than ideal?
   a. Some B&I operations are subsidized.
   b. The existence of satellite outlets.
   c. Inclusion of catering activities.
   d. All of the above.
   e. None of the above.

8. What is the name of the term calculated as the food cost corresponding to a typical midday meal?
   a. Meals per labor hour.
   b. Equivalent meal value (EMV).
   c. Floating equivalent-meal-price factor (EMP).
   d. None of the above.

9. What is the name of the term that refers to the average price of a complete meal specific to the daypart, catered event, or patient meal?
    a. Meals per labor hour.
    b. Equivalent meal value (EMV).
    c. Floating equivalent-meal-price factor (EMP).
    d. None of the above.

10. In total-factor analysis, which two critical measures of quality are integrated as an emerging practice?
    a. Ingredient quality and ingredient price.
    b. Customer satisfaction and employee satisfaction.
    c. Restaurant profit and restaurant rank.
    d. None of the above.

11. Which of the following can be used to express productivity?
    a. Multiple-partial-factor statistic.
    b. Partial-factor statistic.
    c. Both a. and b.
    d. None of the above.

12. Which of the following is indicated by inelastic demand for a foodservice operation's menu offering?
    a. When menu prices are increased, the percentage reduction in the number of items sold is less that the percentage of the price increase.
    b. When prices are raised, the number of corresponding menu items ordered is disproportionately lower.
    c. When menu prices are increased, demand falls to absolute zero.
    d. None of the above.

13. Which of the following is another name for the Pareto principle?
    a. The 80-20 rule.
    b. The law of the vital few.
    c. The principle of factor sparsity.
    d. All of the above.
    e. None of the above.

14. While the total productivity measure is a much more robust statistic than partial-factor productivity statistics are, it still fails to account for an important operational concern. Which of the following is that?
    a. Quality.
    b. Cost.
    c. Output.
    d. None of the above.

15. Which of the following is an important component of patient meals that strongly influences the meals-per-labor-hour determination in healthcare foodservice operations?
    a. Floor stocks.
    b. Dietary supplements.
    c. Between-meal snacks.
    d. All of the above.
    e. None of the above.

Fill in the Blanks

1. Referred to as _____ in years past, revenue management lies at the core of any business.

2. Companies implementing revenue management effectively report up to _____ greater revenue than do those that forgo such techniques.

3. _____ can be manipulated in order to maximize revenue.

4. _____ coupons can entice customers who might not otherwise patronize a foodservice operation.

5. _____ provides a means by which foodservice operators can assess customer sensitivity to menu prices.

6. In segments such as onsite foodservice where multiple dining options exist, demand is generally _____.

7. _____ allows us to view fixed expenses as a direct function of a foodservice operation.

8. A _____ is an expense that is necessitated by a foodservice operation's general processes and is allocated again in proportion to the raw cost of each menu item.

9. In the corrections, education, and healthcare onsite foodservice segments, _____ is a common partial-factor productivity measure.

10. Many healthcare foodservice managers have addressed their revenue management issues by using an _____, calculated as the food cost corresponding to a typical midday meal.

11. _____ analysis using dollar-based statistics must be adjusted to reflect constant-dollar values.

Case in Point: Sales and Labor

Heather was excited about her new job. She had never thought about working in a senior-living facility with a large assisted-living area. In fact, she had thought that 'nursing homes' were places where old people lived and where the employees were old, too. So, when the recruiter called, she was somewhat surprised. However, after the initial interview with the facility administrator, Karl, and the subsequent tour, she had a completely different view of this healthcare segment. The residents were amazing and not everyone was 'old.' Moreover, the other managers and employees seemed fun and energetic; they also seemed to really like what they did for a living. Thus, at only 29 years old, Heather had an opportunity to manage the upscale café as well as the patient services in the facility. It sounded like there might also be some opportunities to cater events.

Rolling Hills was part of a huge chain of assisted-living facilities. Heather viewed this as another advantage. It meant that there would be opportunities for upward mobility—although she wasn't sure what these opportunities might be. Karl had said only that, in terms of organizational structure, she reported directly to him but would also have a dotted-line relationship (called such because that is how it appeared on the organizational chart) with the regional dietitian.

The first few months were challenging but satisfying. Heather managed 22 employees, most of whom worked full time. In her second month, she fired an employee who complained incessantly. Apparently, this employee had other problems, including stealing food from the storeroom. Other than that, things were shaping up nicely. She had also found a great replacement for the fired employee.

During a staff meeting that included all the managers in the facility, the nursing director complimented Heather on the recent cosmetic changes in the café. She then posed a question to Heather: "Why doesn't the café offer cold food to go, such as pizzas that can be cooked at home or pre-cooked chickens? It would be much more convenient for employees to buy food in the café for dinner instead of having to stop at the supermarket."

Heather put the same question to her staff the next morning. Their response was overwhelmingly positive. It turns out that this had been requested many times over the last few years. Unfortunately, the former foodservice director had vehemently opposed the idea.

Heather also had the opportunity to meet Suzanne, the regional dietitian. Suzanne seemed very nice and during their few short meetings told Heather that she was there to support her and that she was available by phone at any time. Suzanne also mentioned that they would review the operating statistics for the foodservice department in the near future.

After six months, it was time for Heather's mid-year review, which was conducted by both Karl and Suzanne. The review began with several compliments, one again about the café. Then, Suzanne explained that corporate had noted a major red flag that deserved Heather's immediate attention. According to a corporate report that compared foodservice operations at all of the Rolling Hills facilities, Heather's foodservice operation was using more labor hours per patient bed than any other was. Suzanne explained that this productivity statistic was monitored closely because it was a good indicator of labor management. After all, it was reasonable that foodservice directors of larger facilities would require more labor, but any differences should be proportional to the number of beds.

Heather let out a sigh of relief. She quickly explained that she had added an FTE three months earlier. This position was responsible for making the numerous 'to go' items now available in the café. The items included, just as the nursing director had requested, pizza and roasted chickens, but the choices didn't stop there. They also offered side dishes such as whipped potatoes with garlic and macaroni and cheese. These were packaged in microwavable containers so people could buy the pre-cooked food and quickly assemble a family meal when they got home. The café had even begun offering cakes and pies, which were extremely popular. Sales in the café had skyrocketed.

Suzanne smiled, but then said: "It's great that you're doing such wonderful things. Karl tells me that the staff really likes the convenience, too. That being said, we are measured on labor hours per patient bed. You are going to have to figure out some way to show the impact of this "take home" program on your organization. Without this, you will not be meeting the company productivity standard. And if you can't get your labor hours below the company standard, we will be forced to find a new foodservice director."

What should Heather do?

Chapter 17: Beverage Management

Learning Objectives

After becoming familiar with this chapter, you should be able to:

1. Appreciate the history of the beverage industry and understand how prohibition affects today's beverage operations.
2. Understand the effects of alcohol on health and the legal issues that affect the sales and service of alcoholic beverages.
3. Explain how managing foodservice operations and pricing food for sale differs from managing alcohol sales and service.
4. Determine training requirements related to beverage service based on a foodservice operation's location and unique features.

Chapter Outline

- Beverage Industry Overview
  - A Brief History
    - As early as 10,000 BC and most likely the result of an accident, humans discovered that food with natural sugar and enough moisture content would ferment into an alcoholic beverage.
    - The Greeks—Viticulture
    - Middle ages—Distillation
    - By the sixteenth century, spirit drinking was still practiced largely for medicinal purposes.
    - Seventeenth century—Sparkling wine
    - By the eighteenth century, the English government was actively promoting gin production to utilize surplus grain and to raise revenue.
    - Gin Epidemic
    - Temperance movement
  - Prohibition
    - Many women supported the anti-alcohol sentiment.
    - The Eighteenth Amendment
    - The National Prohibition Act of 1920

- - The Volstead Act
  - The Noble Experiment
  - The Twenty-First Amendment
  - Bootleggers
  - Today's Beverage Industry (Figures 17.3, 17.4, 17.5)
    - Benefit of beverage sales
    - Trend and lifestyle changes
    - Alcohol consumption in the United States
- Responsible Beverage Alcohol Service
  - Alcohol and Health (Figure 17.6)
    - Ethanol content in various beverages
    - The French paradox
    - Phenolic compounds
    - Subjective or aesthetic benefits
    - Moderation
    - Blood alcohol concentration
  - Legal Issues
    - Duties of care
    - Dramshop laws
    - Foreseeability
    - Reasonable care
- Beverage Control
  - General Guidelines
    - Use a par system.
    - Manage the ordering process.
    - Maintain consistency in recipes.
    - Keep the bar supplied with glassware and ice.
    - Standardize beverage recipes.
  - Purchasing, Receiving, Storing, and Issuing
    - Control vs. license states
    - Brands: well brands, call brands, premium brands, ultra-premium brands

- Four basic steps of receiving:
  - Confirm that the delivery matches the purchase order.
  - Confirm that the invoice matches the purchase order.
  - Make accept-or-reject decisions.
  - Complete the paperwork:
    - Check vintages, bottle sizes, brand, and varieties.
    - Paperwork must take place in a secure environment.
- Storing
  - Ideal temperature varies for different beverages.
  - Ideal humidity varies for different beverages.
  - Spirits should have dedicated space in the storage room and be grouped by type.
  - Use security precautions.
- Issuing
  - Beverage items are typically issued directly from the beverage storage areas to the bar.
  - For spirits, issuing is best facilitated using a one-empty-for-one-full approach.
  - Stamp bottles as they are issued with a unique symbol, perhaps the restaurant logo.
  - Use the par system.
- Pricing
  - Challenges in pricing
  - Varied offerings
  - Gross profit on varied offerings
  - Pricing by the glass
  - Recent trend to offer flights of beer or wine
- Staff Training
  - The Basics
    - Licensing
    - In some states, no unfinished wine can be removed from the premises.

- In other states, unfinished wine can be taken home by the customer after the server replaces the cork and wraps the bottle in a sealed package.
- Some operations charge a corkage fee.
- Legal serving hours
  - Last call
- Minimum age for drinking alcohol
  - Minimizing Liability
    - Ensure public safety.
    - Monitor patrons in the bar.
    - Ensure that no guest is overserved.
    - The National Restaurant Association Educational Foundation
    - The fake ID
      - *The ID Checking Guide*
- Managerial Implications
- Industry Exemplar: M. J. Barleyhoppers
- Case in Point: The Fake ID

Questions for Review

True False Questions

1. T F Ethanol in any form contains an enzyme, the t-PA antigen, which helps prevent chronic internal blood clots.

2. T F Intoxication in most states is a blood alcohol concentration (BAC) of 0.08 percent.

3. T F A foodservice operation that serves alcohol is never held responsible to any extent for the behavior of its customers.

4. T F A critical step in managing the beverage ordering process is recording beverage sales properly.

5. T F When in storage, bottled beer should be protected from sunlight.

6. T F The gross profit on a glass of wine is proportionately lower than it is on a full bottle.

7. T F In some states, no unfinished wine can be removed from the premises.

8. T F Bottled wine typically has the lowest beverage cost percentage.

9. T F It is always easy to distinguish the intoxicated from those who are merely pleasantly disposed or mellow.

10. T F Beverage items are typically issued directly from the beverage storage areas to the bar.

Multiple Choice Questions

1. About how much wine do Americans drink today compared with 1960?
    a. More than two-and-a-half times as much.
    b. About the same.
    c. Less than two-and-a-half times as much.
    d. More than 5 times as much.
    e. None of the above.

2. What antioxidants in wines protect humans against various diseases and the effects of aging?
    a. Ethanol.
    b. Phenolic compounds.
    c. t-PA antigen.
    d. None of the above.

3. According to The National Institute of Alcohol Abuse and Alcoholism, what constitutes "low-risk" drinking for men?
   a. No more than 14 drinks a week with no more than 4 drinks on any given day.
   b. No more than 7 drinks a week with no more than 3 drinks on any given day.
   c. No more than 28 drinks a week with no more than 6 drinks on any given day.
   d. None of the above.

4. According to The National Institute of Alcohol Abuse and Alcoholism, what constitutes "low-risk" drinking for women?
   a. No more than 14 drinks a week with no more than 4 drinks on any given day.
   b. No more than 7 drinks a week with no more than 3 drinks on any given day.
   c. No more than 28 drinks a week with no more than 6 drinks on any given day.
   d. None of the above.

5. Which concept refers to the reasonable anticipation that a particular course of action will likely result in harm or injury?
   a. Dramshop laws.
   b. Foreseeability.
   c. Reasonable care.
   d. Duties of care.

6. For spirits, issuing is best facilitated using which of the following approaches?
   a. A one-empty-for-two-full approach.
   b. A one-empty-for-one-full approach.
   c. A two-empty-for-one-full approach.
   d. None of the above.

7. The typical level of humidity for wine storage is?
   a. 0-10 %.
   b. 30-40%.
   c. Above 70%.
   d. 50-60%.

8. Bottled beer should be kept at temperatures within which of the following ranges?
   a. 0-10 degrees Fahrenheit.
   b. 30–39 degrees Fahrenheit.
   c. Above 70 degrees Fahrenheit.
   d. 40–50 degrees Fahrenheit.

9. What is the name of the compounds/enzymes found in ethanol that helps prevent chronic internal blood clots?
   a. t-PA antigens.
   b. Amino acids.
   c. Phenolic compounds.
   d. None of the above.

10. Which of the following steps is NOT involved in receiving beverages?
    a. Confirming that the delivery matches the purchase order.
    b. Confirming that the invoice matches the purchase order.
    c. Making accept-or-reject decisions.
    d. Tasting to see if the beverage is okay.
    e. Completing the paperwork.

11. Which alcoholic beverage has the lowest cost percentage?
    a. Draft beer.
    b. Spirits.
    c. Bottled beer.
    d. Bottled wine.

12. Which alcoholic beverage has the highest cost percentage?
    a. Draft beer.
    b. Spirits.
    c. Bottled beer.
    d. Bottled wine.

13. What is the typical method used to price wine by the half glass?
    a. Charging the same as for a full glass.
    b. Charging 50% of the price of a full glass.
    c. Charging 10% of the price of a bottle.
    d. Charging 60% of the price of a full glass.

14. What is the name of the fee customers typically need to pay for bringing their own wine into a restaurant?
    a. Gratuity.
    b. Corkage fee.
    c. Last call fee.
    d. Opening fee.

15. Intoxication in most states refers to a blood alcohol concentration (BAC) of what percent?
    a. 0.1.
    b. 0.05.
    c. 0.08.
    d. 1.

16. What is the typical level of par stock used by a beverage service operator?
    a. One-and-a-half times the amount sold during a typical shift.
    b. Twice the amount sold during a typical shift.
    c. The same amount as sold during a typical shift.
    d. Half the amount sold during a typical shift.
    e. None of the above.

17. Which term refers to states in which the foodservice operator must buy liquor from state stores?
    a. Control states.
    b. License states.
    c. Non-regulated states.
    d. None of the above.

18. Which of the following refers to the basic spirits used unless a customer requests a specific brand of alcohol?
    a. Well brands.
    b. Call brands.
    c. Premium brands.
    d. Ultra-premium brands.
    e. None of the above.

19. Of which type of brand is Rémy Martin Louis XIII cognac a good example?
    a. Well brands.
    b. Call brands.
    c. Premium brands.
    d. Ultra-premium brands.
    e. None of the above.

20. Which of the following is not important in receiving beverages?
    a. Checking vintages.
    b. Checking bottle sizes.
    c. Checking brand and varieties.
    d. Carrying out in a secure environment.
    e. None of the above.

21. What is a common practice in pricing house wines served by the bottle in restaurants?
    a. Three times the wholesale price.
    b. One-and-a-half times the wholesale price.
    c. Twice the wholesale price.
    d. None of the above.

Fill in the Blanks

1. In the Middle Ages, the most important innovation regarding alcohol was _____.

2. The _____ was a period of extreme drunkenness that provoked moral outrage and governmental intervention.

3. The _____ was a social movement in which the consumption of alcohol was discouraged and even openly combated.

4. The alcohol responsible for the intoxicating effects of beer, wine, and spirits is _____.

128

5. _____ are antioxidants that protect humans against various diseases and the effects of aging.

6. In many cases, legal liability is related to _____, which is the reasonable anticipation that a particular course of action will result in harm or injury.

7. Typically, the _____ level is one-and-a-half times the amount sold during a typical shift.

8. A _____ is usually the equivalent of a single full serving but the price for this assortment is generally slightly higher than is the price for a single full serving.

9. The _____ allows the server to open and serve wine, while it allows customers perhaps to save money or simply to drink their favorite wine.

10. _____ has served as a social lubricant, fueling economies and stimulating cross-cultural interactions for centuries.

Case in Point: The Fake ID

When Josh's older brother Jake went to college, he quickly found someone who could obtain a fake driver's license for him, enabling him to get into bars near campus. Jake, now in his 30s (the two boys are 15 years apart in age), frequently tells stories of his college shenanigans that were made possible by his premature entry into the bar scene. Jake often adds, at the end of every story, an observation to the effect that using a fake ID "was no big deal. Everyone had one and if you got caught they just slapped your wrist."

It was no surprise, then, that when Josh started college he thought it would be a good idea to get a fake ID.

Times had indeed changed and Josh found that asking around did not produce positive results. In fact, most people to whom he mentioned the idea discouraged it. "Why do you want to get a fake ID?" "Why risk getting kicked out of school?" "We have lots of functions around the college that are fun—why do you need to drink just to have fun?"

These questions made him rethink the whole idea. Still, he kept coming back to his brother's hysterical stories. Josh wanted to have the same kind of college experience that his brother had enjoyed. So he did some online searching and found a site that, for a mere $500, would deliver a falsified driver's license that, according to the site, "even fools trained experts."

Before the first semester was barely underway, Josh got his dream answered in the yellow envelope with no return address. Sure enough, there it was. It didn't look very authentic. It was from another state, however, and since Josh had never seen a driver's license from that state he assumed it was a good rendition.

Friday night came around, and Josh headed out to the best-known pub near campus. He'd never been in the place and was nervous, but he wanted to experience his own stories to tell his friends just as Jake had told him his.

The large, somewhat intimidating bouncer stood at the bar's entrance and when Josh's turn in line finally came, said only: "ID please." Josh was ready with his new ID in hand. It took the bouncer all of three seconds before he responded, "This looks fake. Are you sure you want to use it?"

Josh was crushed. What did he mean 'fake'? He had spent his entire summer savings on the ID; it couldn't look fake! Then the bouncer told him he would call the police to double check. He then gave Josh a choice: "Look, you aren't the first one to try to use a fake ID. And, yes, I'm going to confiscate it. However, if you just walk away, I'll forget I ever saw you and simply put the fake ID in the box with the other hundreds of them that I've collected since I started working here. Or you can wait for just a minute and the police will take care of it."

Josh was so sure that the ID was the real deal that he hadn't thought about what to do if this happened. He was so thunderstruck that he did nothing. He simply stood there. It seemed like only seconds had passed when two police officers began asking him questions. He was then escorted to their patrol car and taken to the station. There, he was booked for a felony.

While in some states using a fake I.D. is still a misdemeanor, other states have equated it to identify fraud and treat it as a felony offense, meaning more jail time, higher fines, and years-long suspensions of driving privileges. Over the long term, a felony weighs down the offender with a criminal record that might limit his or her career choices (a felon cannot qualify for a liquor license, for example). In addition, the offender might be prohibited from owning a gun or voting. Unfortunately, the state where Josh was going to college fell into this latter category.

As a result of the conviction, he was kicked out of school.

What would you have advised Josh to do before he got the fake I.D.? What lessons can you learn from this? (Unfortunately, this is a true story—only the names have been changed . . .)

Chapter 18: The Future of the Foodservice Industry

Learning Objectives

After becoming familiar with this chapter, you should be able to:
1. Apply lessons learned from past changes in the foodservice industry to enhance your understanding of the issues facing managers today.
2. Appreciate the forces that affect and are in many ways shaping the future of foodservice management.
3. Identify likely changes that we will see in each of the foodservice segments.
4. Conceptualize how devices and applications that are typical of today's technology might evolve in tomorrow's foodservice industry.

Chapter Outline

- Lessons from the Past
    - National Restaurant Association identified nine basic functional areas of a foodservice manager's job.
    - Study predicts the skills that managers in the year 2000 would need.
    - *Modern Mechanics* predictions from 1950.
- Forces for Change
    - Globalization
        - McDonaldization
    - Social Responsibility
        - Corporate social responsibility
    - Sustainability
        - Reducing food miles
        - Reducing carbon footprint
        - Use of purchasing and usage
            - Typical energy use in foodservice operations (see Figure 18.2).
        - Common steps that foodservice operations are taking toward a sustainable, green future:
            - Recycling
            - Composting

- Reducing energy
- Reducing water use
- Managing packaging practices
  - Competitive marketing advantages
  - Quest for Quality
    - Foodservice operators must understand consumers' changing attitudes, behaviors, and dining preferences more than ever.
- Predictions by Segment
  - Quick Service
    - There will be greater demand for healthier foods.
    - Trend will be toward greater nutrition disclosure.
    - Hiring good employees will become even more difficult in the future.
    - Pricing models will increasingly differentiate.
  - Fast Casual
    - Continue to grow and will be influenced strongly by cuisines of various cultures.
    - The lines that separate the QSR, fast-casual, and midscale segments will continue to blur.
    - Fast-casual chains will expand into other dayparts, particularly breakfast, and will likely offer lower pricing.
    - Service quality will increase as a differentiating factor, with greater emphasis on customer-employee interaction during food delivery.
    - Human interaction at the point of sale will be reduced as technology emerges in the order-taking process.
  - Family/Midscale
    - A prevailing theme will be increasing customer loyalty.
    - Frequent-user programs will help drive business.
    - Restaurants will be more technology-intensive.
    - Servers will become membership stewards, helping customers become members so they feel as though they belong to an exclusive group.
    - Product and price variation will increase.

- o Moderate/Theme
  - ▪ Integrate many offerings typically found only in fine dining restaurants.
  - ▪ Comfort foods will be different than those usually associated with American cuisine.
  - ▪ Menus will tell a story.
  - ▪ There will be more prix fixe dining options.
  - ▪ Dining duration will increase.
  - ▪ More operations are adopting pervasive themes that transcend every aspect of the restaurant.
- o Fine Dining
  - ▪ Small-portions approach will manipulate psychological barriers to spending.
  - ▪ Fine dining chefs will replace waiters, serving the food themselves throughout a restaurant as opposed to doing so only at the chef's table.
- o Onsite
  - ▪ More and more foodservice operations will be run by managed-services companies.
  - ▪ Trend will be toward healthier menu items.
  - ▪ Food offerings will continue to increase in sophistication in tandem with an increasingly sophisticated customer base.
  - ▪ A greater variety of ethnic dishes will be offered.
  - ▪ There will be greater customization and more choice in menu items.
  - ▪ Vending
    - • Trend will be toward healthier vending machine offerings.
    - • A wider range of food items will be available, including items cooked to order.
    - • Cashless vending will facilitate greater sales.
    - • More technology-intensive design and operation will help shape changes in vending.
- • Technology in 2050

133

- o Extending What Is "New" Today
    - ▪ Tablet computers will be widely used.
        - • Linebusting solution
        - • Training platform
- o Singularity is the concept that bodies and brains will merge with machines.
    - ▪ Accutemp's Flipper the Robocook (see Figure 18.5).
    - ▪ There will be more automation.
- o Final Thought
- • Industry Exemplar: Five Guys Burgers and Fries
- • Case in Point: The Traditional Family-style Restaurant

Questions for Review

True False Questions

1. T F Corporate social responsibility stems from ethical behavior at the individual level.

2. T F Investing in the community is not one of the prime concerns of corporate social responsibility.

3. T F Investors often choose to put their money into companies that share their values and ethics.

4. T F It is predicted that fast casual chains will expand into other dayparts, particularly breakfast, and will offer pricing that will likely capture new customers.

5. T F Dining duration is predicted to increase in the moderate/theme restaurant segment.

6. T F Onsite vending machines are predicted to offer increasingly healthier options.

7. T F McDonald's buys most of its beef locally in an attempt to support local communities.

8. T F Sustainability refers to business practices that contribute to or preserve rather than deplete natural resources.

9. T F Some states in the U.S. allow foodservice operators to buy electricity from third-party suppliers, but too few consider this even though it is typically cheaper.

10. T F Statistics from the U.S. Environmental Protection Agency illustrate that cooking is responsible for 80% of total utility expenses in foodservice operations.

Multiple Choice Questions

1. Which of the following predictions made by early prognosticators did not come true?
   a. An electronic electrical stove will be able to defrost food in seconds.
   b. Sawdust and wood pulp will be converted into sugary foods.
   c. Experts will develop ways of deep-freezing partially baked cuts of meat.
   d. None of the above.

2. Between 1700 and today, the total area of cultivated land worldwide increased almost:
   a. Not at all
   b. 100 percent
   c. 200 percent
   d. 500 percent

3. Which is an effect of sweeping mechanization since the early 1800s?
   a. Agricultural products increased as a percentage of total exports.
   b. Agricultural products decreased as a percentage of total exports.
   c. An increase in the number of farmers due to increased cultivated land.
   d. None of the above.

4. Which is NOT the result of globalization?
   a. The industry is becoming recession proof.
   b. Financial downturns in a country's economy can be covered my operations in other parts of the world.
   c. Leading companies in foodservice are global.
   d. Regional economies and cultures have become more integrated.

5. Which of the following onsite foodservice providers is based in France?
   a. ARAMARK.
   b. Compass Group.
   c. Sodexo.
   d. None of the above.

6. Social responsibility is a force for change because:
   a. It is no longer a fad that companies grudgingly adopt as a marketing vehicle.
   b. It is now a common operating practice.
   c. An organization will naturally attract employees to whom socially responsible business practices are appealing.
   d. All of the above.

7. Sustainability pertains to all but which of the following?
   a. The capacity to endure.
   b. Increasing the carbon footprint.
   c. Business practices that contribute to or preserve natural resources.
   d. Reducing the number of food miles associated with each product used.

8. Which is NOT an approach that will lead to reduced resource usage?
   a. Focusing primarily on reducing gas and electricity for cooking.
   b. Using LED and compact fluorescent bulbs.
   c. Switching to a digital thermostat.
   d. Adopting robust recycling programs.

9. Foodservice operators should make known their green practices because:
   a. Customers will likely choose a restaurant based on its environmental friendliness.
   b. Sustainability practices can help attract and retain good employees who want to work for companies that care about the environment.
   c. Guests find a foodservice operation's energy and water conservation practices appealing.
   d. All of the above.

10. To meet this customer-driven quest for quality, foodservice operators must understand consumers':
    a. Changing attitudes.
    b. Preference for delineated dayparts.
    c. Adversity to bold changes in food and service.
    d. Static dining choices.

11. Singularity is:
    a. A concept borrowed from genetic research.
    b. The notion that a single, complex trend will **pervade** our industry.
    c. The pace of technological change will **become so** rapid that our bodies and our brains will ultimately merge with some sort of **automation** or machination.
    d. Technology will become more consistent in terms of how it is applied in terms of social networks.

Fill in the Blanks

1. McDonald's has become emblematic of _____; some people call it McDonaldization.

2. _____, or the obligation of an organization to behave ethically, stems from ethical behavior at the individual level.

3. _____ denotes business practices that contribute to or preserve rather than deplete natural resources.

4. Two foodservice functions—_____ and usage—provide the best opportunities to reduce carbon use while lowering energy costs.

5. Foodservice operations with large take-out components should review their _____ practices.

6. Customers can expect to see more _____ dining options in upscale restaurants.

7. Robust _____ programs that include glass, plastics, metals, papers, and cardboard can reduce garbage and the associated refuse removal expense by 50–70%.

8. The National Restaurant Association reports that 62% of adults will likely choose a restaurant based on its _____.

9. Foodservice professionals who are bold and willing to take risks on innovative _____ will likely realize huge returns.

10. The easy prediction for QSRs based on current trends is that _____ will continue to fall out of favor.

Case in Point: The Traditional Family-style Restaurant

Edward had seen it all. When he got his first foodservice job in college, things were simple. The foodserver took the customers' orders, entered them in the POS terminal by the condiment station, and then delivered the food when the cooks finished preparing it. Some 40 years later, Edward couldn't even remember the last time he had hired a foodserver. In place of the traditional dining-room manager was now a woman with a degree in information systems and a minor in business. Most of her days were spent ensuring that the automated order system embedded in the surface of each table was functioning within expected parameters. The system was responsible for changing menu items and the associated holographic display (along with prices) depending on the level of business, the demographic of the customers seated at a particular table, the time of day, and the cost of items calculated in real time as they arrived in the kitchen.

Edward looked over the dining room and thought, "What has happened to the food*service* business?" The food at his typical family-style restaurant was delivered to each table via a series of belts and sophisticated automated robotics once found only in automotive assembly plants. The bar still featured an attractive display of fancy liquor bottles, but the actual beverages were made by a machine and delivered in the same way as the food. Guests didn't even expect a person to clear their dishes; they had long become accustomed to using the "back window," a hatch of sorts found at each table through which dirty dishes were deposited by the customer and then automatically sanitized and returned to the kitchen for reuse.

Missing the days of old, Edward espied a table of older customers and decided to surprise them by personally delivering their food. He thought they would be thrilled. He couldn't have been more wrong.

When he arrived at the table, the guests looked at him as if he was some sort of thief, or perhaps someone who might have tainted their food. The woman closest to Edward said, "Thank you, but we'll wait for our food to be delivered the usual way." She then resumed her conversation with her friends.

Edward returned to his office. He had originally gone into the foodservice business because he liked serving people. He always had a great feeling when guests were pleasantly surprised by a creative dish or a wine that they had never had but thanks to the sommelier's suggestion would now be their new favorite. This was a people business.

He couldn't help but wonder, "Would things ever return to the way they were in the good old days?"